A BRIEF GENEALOGY OF JEWISH REPUBLICANISM

BEFORE YOU START TO READ THIS BOOK, take this moment to think about making a donation to punctum books, an independent non-profit press,

@ https://punctumbooks.com/support/

If you're reading the e-book, you can click on the image below to go directly to our donations site. Any amount, no matter the size, is appreciated and will help us to keep our ship of fools afloat. Contributions from dedicated readers will also help us to keep our commons open and to cultivate new work that can't find a welcoming port elsewhere. Our adventure is not possible without your support.

Vive la open-access.

Fig. 1. Hieronymus Bosch, *Ship of Fools* (1490–1500)

First published in 2016 by dead letter office, BABEL Working Group
an imprint of punctum books, Earth, Milky Way.
https://punctumbooks.com

The BABEL Working Group is a collective and desiring-assemblage of scholar–gypsies with no leaders or followers, no top and no bottom, and only a middle. BABEL roams and stalks the ruins of the post-historical university as a multiplicity, a pack, looking for other roaming packs with which to cohabit and build temporary shelters for intellectual vagabonds. We also take in strays.

ISBN-13: 978-0-9982375-9-6
ISBN-10: 0-9982375-9-0
Library of Congress Cataloging Data is available from the Library of Congress

Book design: Vincent W.J. van Gerven Oei

Irene Tucker

A Brief Genealogy of

Jewish Republicanism

Parting Ways
with Judith Butler

Acknowledgments

In addition to the wise counsel of the press's two anonymous readers, I'm grateful to the following friends and colleagues for a range of stimulating conversations that helped shape this piece, and especially for their willingness to contemplate positions that might not be precisely their own: Aaron Alexander, Ayelet Ben-Yishai, Sharon Brous, David Clark, Elizabeth Maddock Dillon, Nir Evron, Stanley Fish, Sharon Gillerman, Evan Gottlieb, Daniel Gross, Jonathan Grossman, Neil Hertz, Chris Hoeckley, Oren Izenberg, Tamar Katz, Alexander Kaye, Arlene Keizer, Cheri Larsen Hoeckley, Rachel Rubinstein, Hilary Schor, Milette Shamir, Jeffrey Shoulson, Geetanjali Srikantan, Yael Sternhell, Nomi Stolzenberg, Dvora Weisberg, Sarah Winter, Hana Wirth-Nesher, and Amit Yahav. I'm thankful too for having had the opportunity to present earlier versions at the English and American Studies faculty seminar of Tel Aviv University, as well as the lunchtime seminar of the USC Center for Law, History and Culture.

Special thanks to Lauren Berlant, for her generosity and imaginativeness in the service of the not insignificant task of finding a publishing venue for this piece; Vincent van Gerven Oei, for his unusual ability to combine the skills of editor and cover artist; and to Eileen Joy for her fierceness, intellectual integrity, and fearlessless in bringing into being sensible and humane practices and institutions of academic publishing.

A Brief Genealogy of
Jewish Republicanism

Parting Ways with
Judith Butler

On January 22, 2013, Israeli citizens headed to the polls to elect the nineteenth Knesset, or Parliament. So confident was the sitting Prime Minister, Benjamin Netanyahu, of the continuing public support for his platform, which included increasingly alarmist rhetoric about the dangers posed to Israel by Iran's secret nuclear program, that he called elections eight months ahead of schedule. For the previous three years, Netanyahu's focus on Iran had functioned to draw the attention of Jewish Israelis away from the long-simmering issues surrounding Israel's occupation of the Palestinian territories, and the generally held expectation was that a strong showing by the shared list of his just-formed right-wing unity coalition Likud–Yisrael Beitenu might function to authorize a preemptive Israeli military strike against Iran's nuclear facilities, and so continue Netanyahu's tactical politics of distraction.

When the polls closed that night, politicians and analysts alike were stunned to discover that the electorate had swung decidedly to the left. The day's results suggested that voters were animated by a host of issues not limited to security and the occupation but extending to questions of economic justice and the equitable distribution of national service. By the time the final votes were tabulated, Netanyahu's unity list found itself eleven seats down from its standing total in the just-dissolved government. Because this array of voter commitments did not fall neatly along the lines laid out by the party platforms of Israel's notoriously fragmented electoral system, Netanyahu was forced to negotiate for nearly two months — past one deadline and only days from a second — to form the parliamentary majority necessary to allow him to continue to govern.[1]

---

1   Despite the shift in voters' positions, the coalition ultimately assembled has not governed in a significantly more progressive way, either on economic issues or on matters of peace, than Netanyahu's previous government. This disjunction between the shift of voter sentiment and the relative stasis of the governing position has been largely the consequence of the partnership established as a condition of entry into the government between the leaders of two apparently politically divergent parties — the center-left Yesh Atid (There is a Future) party of Yair Lapid, and the far-right, ultra-nationalist, HaBayit HaYehudi (Jewish Home) party of Naftali Bennett. Nevertheless, recent scholarly surveys seem to support the conclusion that a large majority of Yesh Atid voters (Yesh Atid was the biggest beneficiary of the election's leftward shift) were motivated to vote for the party on the basis of its support for the establishment of a Palestinian state, and that they chose Lapid's newly established party because they imagined it might break through the stalemate of already-familiar party positions. See Yonaton Lees, "Sof haMercaz Smola" ("End of the Center Left"), *Haaretz* (Hebrew) Nov. 22, 2013, 7 (print). Although I've chosen to focus on the 2013 election for its serendipitous proximity to Butler's appearance and remarks at Brooklyn College and the controversy surrounding that appearance, in the more recent 2015 election, a similar disjunction emerged between trends in voter sentiment and the ultimate orientation of the assembled government. While the left picked up three additional seats, the very narrow, one-seat majority ultimately assembled by Prime Minister Benjamin Netanyahu was even more rightist than the previous government. But Netanyahu himself seemed alive to the political power — or threat — of diverse coalitions: his notoriously racist exhortation to right-leaning Jewish voters to vote for his Likud party to counterbalance the "droves of Arab voters" coming to the polls had the effect of consolidating right-wing voters under a single party against the threat of a diverse coalition of center-left and Israeli Arab voters. The newly formed "Joint List," a coalition of normally discrete — and often contentious — parties devoted to representing the disparate interests of Israeli Arab voters garnered enough votes to make it the third largest party in the current Knesset. Nevertheless, the fact that the second largest party (a party of the center-left) had opted to call itself the Zionist Union, had the effect of placing it beyond the pale as a possible coalition partner of the Joint List.

   One of the goals of the essay that follows is to delineate a tradition of Jewish publicness in which the formation of heterogeneous — which is to say, among other things, not exclusively Jewish — coalitions is a crucial component. By delineating such a tradition within a Jewish civic practices, I mean to make a case for a political and conceptual continuity between coalition politics and a two-state solution to the Israeli–Palestinian conflict, as well challenge the relegation of binational alternatives to the margins

Just over two weeks after Israelis cast their ballots and well before coalition negotiations had concluded, Judith Butler addressed an audience at a conference at Brooklyn College organized by that campus's political science department and its branch of Students for Justice in Palestine, and offered, among other rhetorical ventures, a rousing defense of academic freedom. Butler was moved to open her talk in support of the Boycott, Divestment, and Sanctions (BDS) movement with a brief on the intellectual and political value of free argument because her appearance at Brooklyn College along with BDS movement founding organizer Omar Barghouti had already been, for weeks, the object of controversy. Prominent New York City politicians had signed a letter to Brooklyn College's president expressing their concern "that an academic department has decided to formally endorse an event that advocates strongly for one side of a highly-charged issue," and asking that the departmental endorsement be withdrawn.[2] Because Brooklyn College is part of the City University of New York (CUNY) system and receives much of its funding from the city, the letter carried with it an implicit threat to which Butler responded in the opening of her remarks:

---

of Zionist intellectual history. As I hope will become clear, the tradition I outline understands the motivation behind heterogeneous coalitions to be epistemological as well as interest-based. Such coalitions would be designed to allow its members to understand the political, social, and economic environments they inhabit multiply, not simply to exchange favors in relation to preexisting interests. While it is beyond the scope of this essay to delineate the sort of mechanisms that might maintain such epistemological heterogeneity as a central element of the legislative process, the sobering examples of recent coalitions offer a pressing reminder of the importance of deploying or creating such mechanisms.

2   Quoted in Natasha Lennard, "'Effective' censorship over Israel event at Brooklyn College," *Salon*, Feb. 4, 2013. Several months earlier, the municipal leaders of the city of Frankfurt had likewise come under fire for announcing its plans to award Butler its Theodor Adorno prize, an award whose charge is to recognize someone whose achievements in critical theory and engagements with art and music resonated with Adorno's own, a mandate Butler clearly fulfilled. City officials held admirably fast to their commitment to award Butler the prize, despite considerable pressure from Jewish community organizations within Frankfurt.

The principle of academic freedom is designed to make sure that powers outside the university, including government and corporations are not able to control the curriculum or intervene in extra-mural speech. It not only bars such interventions, but it also protects those platforms in which we might be able to reflect together on the most difficult problems.

Butler's elaboration of this point is particularly forceful:

What precisely are we doing here this evening? I presume that you came to hear what there is to be said, and so to test your preconceptions against what some people have to say, to see whether your objections can be met and your questions answered. In other words, you come here to exercise critical judgment, and if the arguments you hear are not convincing, you will be able to cite them, to develop your opposing view and to communicate that as you wish. In this way, your being here this evening confirms your right to form and communicate an autonomous judgment, to demonstrate why you think something is true or not, and you should be free to do this without coercion and fear. These are your rights of free expression, but they are, perhaps even more importantly, your rights to education, which involves the freedom to hear, to read and to consider any number of viewpoints as part of an ongoing public deliberation on this issue. Your presence here, even your support for the event, does not assume agreement among us. There is no unanimity of opinion here; indeed, achieving unanimity is not the goal.[3]

Butler's point here is clear: once government officials are granted — or seize — the power to determine what sorts of arguments are admissible to academic conversations, then those conversations are likely to be directed in ways that serve the preexisting

3   "Judith Butler's Remarks to Brooklyn College on BDS," *The Nation*, Feb. 8, 2013.

political interests of those government officials. The moment academic discussions and the institutional structures in which those discussions take place are used to confirm rather than "to test preconceptions against what some people have to say," then those discussions and those institutional spaces cease to function as "platforms in which we might be able to reflect together on the most difficult problems." Advocates for academic freedom make the mistake of assuming that what is most threatened by the effort to include or exclude participants based on where they are located in some "extra-mural" political sphere is the expressive freedom of the discussion's participants; what is more fundamentally under attack, Butler insists, is the right of interlocutors and listeners alike to learn from the rigor of unstraitened debate.[4]

So it comes as something of a surprise that, when she turns from responding to the controversy surrounding her appearance to the substance of the day's presentation itself — the case to be made for the use of academic and economic boycotts, sanctions, and divestment as strategies for ending the Israeli occupation — Butler offers a markedly different description of the nature of the relations brought into being by the back-and-forth of academic conversation. Responding to charges that criticism of Israeli state policy toward the Palestinians ought to be understood as a form of anti-Semitism, Butler asks:

Why would a non-violent movement to achieve basic political rights for Palestinians be understood as anti-Semitic? Surely, there is nothing about the basic rights themselves that constitute a problem. [...] Why would a collective struggle to use economic and cultural forms of power to compel the enforcement of international laws be considered anti-Semitic?[5]

4 For a wide-ranging, if selective, survey of the various discursive histories of debates over academic freedom, including a brief foray into the contemporary BDS movement, see Akeel Bilgrami and Jonathan Cole, eds., *Who's Afraid of Academic Freedom?* (New York: Columbia University Press, 2015).

5 "Judith Butler's Remarks to Brooklyn College on BDS," *The Nation*, Feb. 8, 2013.

Here the sphere of academic conversation in which autonomous judgment is exercised and honed is redescribed, absent any explanation, as the locus of "cultural forms of power," power that is justly exercised in the service of the admirable — and inarguably political — project of "the enforcement of international laws." Once this redescription has taken place, the relevant criterion of evaluation shifts as well: from the issue of whether the sphere enables the honing of autonomous judgment necessary for discovering new ways of understanding "the most difficult questions" to the issue of whether a given expression is anti-Semitic, or, more implicitly, whether the power of the cultural sphere is power well-exercised.

It might appear, from this opening, as if my angle of encounter with Butler's argument is to show the way in which her engagement with the putative anti-Semitism of the BDS movement, even to dispute those charges, functions as a kind of feint. If Butler insists that right-wing supporters of Israel invoke the supposed anti-Semitism of BDS and other movements critical of the Israeli occupation in order to divert attention from various forms of bad behavior of the Israeli state that are legitimate objects of critique — and surely she's not wrong to make such a claim — a case can equally well be made that Butler's own focus on the question of BDS's anti-Semitism operates to draw attention away from the fundamental incoherence of her position on the wisdom and value of academic boycotts. Such a position simultaneously argues for the need to preserve a sphere in which the measure of a participant's value lies in his or her capacity to contribute to the rigorous testing of the preconceptions of participants and listeners alike and at the same time advocates the preemptive exclusion of certain scholars from such conversations in virtue of "extra-mural" aspects of their identities such as citizenship or association with certain academic institutions.

While I do understand the values articulated by the idea of an academic boycott to be in fatal contradiction with one another, and oppose Butler's — and the BDS movement's — calls for boycott for precisely that reason, neither the logic nor the political wisdom of academic boycott is my primary focus here.[6] The two versions of the academic sphere Butler sets out — on the one hand, as a place, or process, for the testing of opposed ideas and the honing of judgment; on the other, as an instrument of cultural and political power — imply very different structures of subjectivity or agency. Where the former is of necessity both collective and heterogeneous — the multiplicity and heterogeneity of points-of-view are both defining characteristics — the version of the academic sphere that might be wielded as an instrument of power presupposes that whatever multiplicity that exists can — and, at times, ought to — be consolidated into some form of expressive unity. It is the distinction between these two different structures that I believe offers a framework for understanding not simply the argument for BDS (and the right to advocate for it) Butler put forth at Brooklyn College in February 2013, but

---

6   My case for the incoherence of the BDS platform applies only to its position on academic boycotts. Because free and equal access to particular exchanges in an economic market is in no way constitutive of the functioning of that market (indeed, one could argue that differential access to products is an essential aspect of the value of those products), an economic boycott does not violate the fundamental terms of the economic market exchange. Gideon Levy has recently made a persuasive case for the efficacy — and thus the political necessity — of an economic boycott as an instrument for motivating Israel's current market-centric political leadership to take the necessary steps to negotiate the end to the Israeli occupation. See Gideon Levy, "The Israeli Patriot's Final Refuge: Boycott," *Haaretz* (English), July 14, 2013 (electronic edition).

More pragmatically, the Israeli left is by most accounts disproportionately located in universities, and their power to effect change within Israeli political culture and Israeli society at large arguably benefits from the global institutional connections many scholars have developed. Netanyahu's own openly acknowledged hostility to university culture within Israel makes it unlikely that he or the appointed members of his cabinet would be moved to alter their policies because of any external threat to that university culture. Moreover, departments of English at Israeli universities, which have been especially affected by academic boycotts thus far, conduct their courses in English, thereby creating an institutional space within Israeli universities in which the hegemony of the Hebrew language is minimized, if not entirely eliminated. English departments have historically enrolled Israeli Arab students at rates much greater than their enrollment in the universities as a whole, anywhere from twenty to forty percent of all English majors.

the logic and the analytical limitations of the more general critique of Zionism at the heart of Butler's 2013 monograph *Parting
Ways: Jewishness and the Critique of Zionism* as well.

In this more extended work, Butler assembles a formidable
array of Jewish thinkers, devoting individual chapters to closely
argued engagements with writings of Immanuel Levinas, Walter
Benjamin, Hannah Arendt, and Primo Levi, in an effort to produce an ethical–spiritual post-war genealogy of Jewishness. But
for all the subtlety of the individual chapters, what is remarkable
about *Parting Ways* is how little either the specific arguments
that these individual authors present or the particular analyses
Butler makes of them matters to the book's overarching argument. Butler's is a book whose argument rests almost entirely
upon the frame it presents. As I hope will become apparent, the
critique of Zionism offered by *Parting Ways* rises and falls on the
book's demonstration of the general fact that the Jewish thinkers represented within have articulated ambivalence, hostility,
or opposition to some form of state-based Jewish national identity that might be located under the rubric of "Zionism,"[7] or to
the form of the state more generally construed. In some senses,
this assertion that not all Jews embrace the premises of Zionism — or, at bumped up one level of abstraction, that Judaism
and Zionism are non-identical — is an obvious claim masquerading as a revolutionary one. In his 1990 *Jews Against Zionism*,
Thomas Kolsky detailed at considerable length the extensive efforts opposing Zionism mounted by Reform Judaism's "American Council for Judaism" between 1942 and 1948. Numerous
critics of *Parting Ways* have noted Butler's failure to engage or
even account for the ideologically heterogeneous body of writings by Zionist thinkers ranging from Theodor Herzl and Micah
Joseph Berdichevsky to Martin Buber and Vladimir Jabotinsky.[8]

---

7   Judith Butler, *Parting Ways: Jewishness and the Critique of Zionism* (New
    York: Columbia University Press, 2012), 3. Henceforth, *PW.*
8   Thomas A. Kolsky, *Jews Against Zionism: The American Council for Judaism,
    1942–1948* (Philadelphia: Temple University Press, 1990). On Butler's failure
    to engage the ideological diversity of Zionist politics and writing, see Zachary Braiterman, "No *Parting Ways*: The Crypto-Zionism of Judith Butler,"

But simply registering the self-evidence of Butler's claim illuminates little if we don't also analyze the way the assertion of the non-identity of Judaism and Zionism functions in her book's argument and trace the discursive history undergirding such a claim. At the center of *Parting Ways* is a chapter entitled "Is Judaism Zionism?" (a related, though not precisely identical query, to the one structuring her Brooklyn College address: "Is anti-Zionism anti-Semitism?"). To the degree that her assemblage of writers and writings functions to pry apart the two terms, Butler understands the work of critique to be largely accomplished. But the notion that simply demonstrating that Jews can be non- or anti-Zionist too is sufficient to prove that the non- or anti-Zionist position cannot be anti-Jewish relies upon a logic in which beliefs operate like identities. By this logic, the value of a belief lies in the fact that it is the expression of a particular individual, and belief becomes the stuff of individual subjectivity. This mutual constitution of subject and belief effectively renders each unitary and synchronic, and it is this treatment of belief as if it is a kind of unitary identity that most closely follows the logic underlying Butler's advocacy of academic boycotts, a mandate by which the realm of intellectual debate and the testing of ideas are transmuted into an undivided instrument of cultural power.

In opening by drawing attention to the near-coincidence of Butler's controversial appearance at Brooklyn College and the surprise outcome of the Israeli elections, my aim is not to make a claim for the robustness of Israeli democracy, or to suggest that the protracted conflict will surely fix itself, if only the Israeli electorate is left to its own devices. The election was marked by two not entirely predictable, and seemingly contradictory, out-

---

371–77, at 371–72, and Sarah Hammerschlag, "Outside the Canon: Judith Butler and the Trials of Jewish Philosophy," 367–70, at 368, both in *Political Theology* 16, no. 4, Special Issue: Forum on Judith Butler's *Parting Ways* (2015). In response to repeated criticisms of her failure to engage the Zionist intellectual tradition, Butler has, by her own account, begun to engage the work of Martin Buber, a thinker who imagined a Zionism culminating in a binational state resembling the sort that Butler herself advocates. Judith Butler, "Response," *Political Theology* 16, no. 4 (2015): 392–99.

comes: an electorate that defied most professional forecasts by moving decidedly to the left on peace and economic issues, and a coalition that consolidated its governing position markedly to the right of the electorate's distribution and has been responsible for directing the Israeli state's recent brutalities in the occupied territories. Central to a model of political republicanism that directly links the business of governing to voters' acts of self-representation, these two intertwined contingencies — citizens' casting ballots for a given party; the parties' assemblage into a ruling coalition — can be seen, I mean to argue, as variations on the forms historically to have organized some of the defining qualities of Jewish collective life. I introduce the chance synchronicity of the Israeli election and Butler's Brooklyn College address in the hope that it might offer an opening for taking up the same general set of questions Butler does — what has been, is, or ought be the relation between Jewishness and state-centered forms of self-governance? — from within an alternative genealogy more attentive to the specificity of Jewish conceptions of communal life and the proper relations of actions and ideas.

My goal here is not to offer yet another salvo in the all-too-predictable back-and-forth of pro- and anti-BDS talking points that has come to characterize the debate over the past several years. In fact, I understand this essay to be only tangentially related to the BDS debate, at least in the narrowest and most familiar senses in which the terms of the debate are conceived. What I am hoping to do here is to offer a framework for thinking about a longer history of Jewish civic and public organization, as well as to detail a range of ways of thinking about relations of identity and belief. I also mean to demonstrate the ways in which the interconnections of these frameworks allow us to see some of the most polarizing aspects of the BDS debate as part of a complex and longstanding discursive history. My hope is that the analytical reframing I offer will allow BDS combatants to be less combative and more imaginative, not only in discovering points of commonality, but in thinking about how such points of commonality might offer grounds for new sorts of political interventions that might allow for a peaceful resolution of the all-too-protracted and brutal conflict in Israel/Palestine.

I aim to address two distinct audiences. The first group, students and readers of Butler, operates from the premise that Judaism and republicanism are fundamentally at odds with one another. For these readers and thinkers, to embrace state-centered forms of political autonomy is to betray the essential ethical tradition of Judaism. In addition to such avowed anti-Zionists, I mean to address a second audience. These readers do not oppose out of hand the idea of a sovereign state to organize and protect a Jewish public. Although such readers do not necessarily reject the most broadly conceived notions of Zionism in principle, they nevertheless have severe ethical and political misgivings about the practices that have developed in the current state of Israel, particularly those regarding both its treatment of its Arab citizens and its ongoing occupation of Palestinian territories. For this second audience, a commitment to realizing Jewish political sovereignty can at times seem to exist in some degree of tension with a commitment to democracy.

In throwing light on a genealogy of Jewish practices aimed at the deliberate creation of collectives constituted by their grappling with contingent, historical time, I intend to make a case for the existence of a *Jewish tradition of republicanism,* of democracy. Within such a context, the Jewishness of Israel can be seen to lie first and foremost in its methods of generating a civil collective out of a diverse citizenry rather than in the identities of its individual citizens.[9] The tradition I have in mind explicitly

---

9 In invoking the term republicanism, I draw on Michael Sandel's distinction between individualist liberalism and republicanism: "Central to republican theory is the idea that liberty depends on sharing in self-government. This idea is not by itself inconsistent with liberal freedom. Participating in politics can be one among the ways in which people choose to pursue their ends. According to republican political theory, however, sharing in self-rule involves something more. It means deliberating with fellow citizens about the common good and helping to shape the destiny of the political community. But to deliberate well about the common good requires more than the capacity to choose one's ends and to respect others' rights to do the same. It requires knowledge of public affairs and also a sense of belonging, a concern

uses an idea of ritual or "ceremonial law" to sustain within itself a tension between a heterogeneity of perspectives and interests constitutive of democratic process and the forms of unity and agreement often understood to be the desired outcome of that process. By setting forth a framework in which heterogeneity and agreement are conceived as coincident modes of political being rather than steps in a linear process, this "Jewish republicanism" frames the making, implementation, and following of the law as forms of a single structure of ritual practice. Such a framework might provide the inspiration and authority for reconceiving some of the fundamental relations of the Zionist project. In recovering this tradition of public law from within a body of ritual practices most often seen as irrelevant to modern conceptions of state sovereignty, I hope to narrow the conceptual gap between "diasporic" and "Zionist" conceptions of communal life, such that the "Jewishness" of Israel can be both reimagined and reorganized not as the ethnocracy it threatens to become, but rather as the most recent historical instantiation of a contingently heterogeneous collective organized around common — and continuously reinterpretable — law. Such republicanism would not only offer a framework for coexistence in Israel/Palestine, but also would provide a way of reimagining the relations of democratic citizenship and governance more broadly.

It is worth noting that the logic I have been drawing attention to in Butler's argument for boycott, and which I am here calling an identitarian model of belief, also has a formidably longstanding, if very different, historical pedigree from that of Jewish republicanism. A version of Butler's identitarianism can be seen to structure what has come to be the default understanding of secularism in the contemporary United States: the notion that "religion" consists of a set of ideas about the origin and ordering of the world that an individual holds in his or her head, and that a properly secular government is one that remains studi-

---

for the whole, a moral bond with the community whose fate is at stake."
Michael Sandel, *Democracy's Discontent: America in Search of a Public Philosophy* (Cambridge: Harvard University Press, 1996), 5.

ously neutral toward the various contents of these ideas. John Locke has long been recognized as one of the most influential theorists of modern secularism, and I will turn later to his 1689 "Letter on Toleration" in order to parse the logic of the identitarian model of belief that is both his and Butler's.[10] I read Locke's "Letter" in relation to two texts — *The Second Treatise of Government*, Locke's own theory of the origin of property and of the state, and Jewish philosopher Moses Mendelssohn's late-18th-century engagement with Locke's "Letter," *Jerusalem, or On Religious Power and Judaism* (1783) — to suggest the degree to which both Locke and his critics conceived of this individuated "identitarian" model of belief as a response to, rather than an escape from, the pressing political and economic issues of the day. Accordingly, when Mendelssohn rejects Locke's hard-and-fast distinction between the temporal world of state-protected private property and the eternal world in favor of relations of ritual and social engagement he calls "ceremonial law," he is not merely inviting us to attend to the differences between Christian and Jewish understandings of religiosity. In offering a vision of religious practice that is public, collective, and rule-bound, Mendelssohn describes a Jewishness in which civic life and what we might term "religious practice" are indistinguishable from one another. Such an account fundamentally challenges Butler's

---

10 In her 2005 book, *The Impossibility of Religious Freedom* (Princeton: Princeton University Press), Winnifred Fallers Sullivan makes the case that the alignment of "religion" per se with forms of individual belief is a particularly American phenomenon, a seemingly paradoxical consequence of the US constitutional tradition of defining religious liberty as the government's non-endorsement of religious institutions. Sullivan explains: "Unlike in many European countries where religious communities must register with the government, no limits are placed in the United States on the creation of new religious communities." Because "religion" can mean whatever individual believers understand it to mean, courts are placed in an untenable position. "On the one hand they are required by the use of the word 'religion' in statutes and in the Constitution to inquire into its meaning, to draw lines between 'religion' and not-'religion.' On the other hand, there is much law in the United States saying that judges cannot enter into disputes regarding religious orthodoxy. The definition of religion for legal purposes in this country remains, as a result, profoundly unsettled."

contention that the emphasis on publicness and self-determination that characterizes many versions of Zionism marks a radical departure from the models of Jewishness that pre-date Zionism.

This pointedly iterative quality of Mendelssohn's ceremonial law—practices become meaningful both as repetitions of past actions and as transformations of those actions impelled by the shifting historical contexts and populations—might be read as an early model of what political theorist Seyla Benhabib has recently termed "jurisgenerative politics," a not-exclusively-statist model of politics in which the repeated iteration of rights becomes a means both of transforming those rights and of extending them to previously excluded groups. By reading Mendelssohn's account of ceremonial law in relation to a selection of rabbinic sources that are generally taken as the grounds for both the collectivism and the historicism of Jewish ceremonial law, however, I mean to make available a history of Jewish practice (including the fundamental demand for collective prayer known as the *minyan*) in which a republican form of democracy is a longstanding and essential element. Within this context of a history of Jewish republicanism, I hope to show, the extension of Israeli democracy to groups not currently fully represented would not only transform the landscape of the seemingly intractable conflict within Israel/Palestine, but might also provide a framework by which to understand the goal of democratic processes as something other than a stripping away of diversity of opinion. Such a framework invites us to understand the relations of the legislative and executive functions of government as essential and ongoing forms of political expression rather than a structure by which political agreements are struck and then institutionalized.

❧❧❧

IN ITS ESSENCE, BUTLER'S ARGUMENT in *Parting Ways* goes something like this: if Zionism and Judaism are not identical to one another, then critiques — even outright rejections — of Zionism need not be construed as forms of anti-Semitism. But if this reduction stands as a fair summary of Butler's argument, it is not all we stand to learn from or about her claims. The specific language Butler uses to insist upon the distinguishability of Zionism and Judaism matters: her syntactic choices work to construe the force she attributes to the social identities of the authors she analyzes and the shifting verb tenses she introduces function to describe the objects of her inquiry and to establish her own analytical authority. I suggested in my introductory remarks that Butler's presumption that people's ideas can be straightforwardly aligned with their identities can be seen to borrow from foundational Christian conceptions of belief around which modern notions of secularism are organized. By attending to the details of her language, I hope not only to strengthen the case for understanding the location of Butler's work within this discourse of Christian secularism, but also to use the dynamics articulated by her specific linguistic choices as an analytical framework that throws into visibility aspects of secularism and its relations to notions of historicism, private property, and collective sovereignty, and which might otherwise go unnoticed.

As Butler tells it in the opening of *Parting Ways*, over the course of her book's writing, she discovers herself to be faced with a different project than the one on which she embarked:

> What started as a book seeking to debunk the claim that any and all criticism of the State of Israel is effectively anti-Semitic has become a meditation on the necessity of tarrying with the impossible. If I succeed in showing that there are Jewish resources for the criticism of state violence, the colonial subjugation of populations, expulsion and dispossession, then I will have managed to show that a Jewish critique of Israeli state violence is at least possible, if not ethically obligatory. (*PW*, 1)

And if the nature of the impossibility with which Butler finds herself, quite unexpectedly, forced to tarry is not immediately self-evident, she hastens to explain:

> If I win the point on these terms, I am immediately confronted, however, with another problem. By claiming there is a significant Jewish tradition affirming modes of justice and equality that would, of necessity, lead to a criticism of the Israeli state, I establish a Jewish perspective that is non-Zionist, even anti-Zionist at the risk of making even the resistance to Zionism into a "Jewish" value and so asserting, indirectly, the exceptional ethical resources of Judaism. (*PW*, 2)

While her cast of characters is familiar, in *Parting Ways*, in marked contrast with much of Butler's earlier writings, the mere fact of the presence of writers like Levinas, Benjamin, and Arendt is far more essential than the details of their arguments, or of the particulars of Butler's arguments about them. Put most simply, what matters most about these writings is that their authors are Jewish. Positions that might be deemed anti-Semitic or anti-Jewish turn out not to be — so long as the thinkers who articulate or advance those critiques are themselves Jewish.

The essentialism implicit in this straightforward alignment of the public identities of authors with their writing would seem an odd claim even coming from someone whose oeuvre were less identified with laying waste to stable forms of identity, but it is particularly odd coming from Butler. [11] (In this regard, the

---

11 We ought not be surprised that Butler herself seems not entirely comfortable with the identitarian logic undergirding her frame, given her longstanding commitments to versions of non-sovereign, heteronomous forms of subjectivity. In what appears an effort to soften the starkness of this identitarianism, Butler refers to "Jewish resources," but never offers a definition that would give us reason to understand the meaning of Jewish resources as anything other than "texts written by Jews." In her response to the *Political Theology* forum on *Parting Ways,* Butler makes an effort to insist upon a more nuanced conception of the "Jewishness" of her critique of Zionism: "I am asking two sorts of questions that take up the Jewish/Non-Jewish question. When I criticize the state of Israel, am I criticizing that state as a Jewish

reference to "Jewish resources" appears as much an evasion as a claim, a symptom of Butler's own discomfort with the conflation upon which her book's argument turns.) But if the particular quality of Butler's "tarrying with the impossible" remains elusive, the alternative "problem she must subsequently confront" offers a way out of this identitarian conundrum. The "impossibility" she laments appears on first glance to be lamentable in virtue of its conflation of Jews and their resources: by "claiming there is a significant Jewish tradition affirming modes of justice and equality" she runs the risk "of making even the resistance to Zionism into a 'Jewish' value and so asserting [...] the exceptional ethical resources of Jewishness." The risk, that is, is that the tradition affirming justice and equality will be valued not because it is an ethical tradition worthy of value, but because it is a Jewish tradition. But the paradox she identifies is a false

person. After all, I am a Jewish person, and that is not really debatable. But do I understand and designate the position from which I criticize that state as a Jewish position. On the one hand, I do identify in that way and organize my political views partially in relation to that form of belonging. I belong to *Jewish Voice for Peace*, and it is important for me to belong to a Jewish organization that shares and supports many of my views, and where I can support others who have taken positions that potentially ostracize them from some parts of the Jewish community. But am I 'totalized' by my position as a Jew? In fact, many of the arguments I make are made by others who are not Jewish, and they have to do with fundamental convictions that are shared regarding equal rights of citizenship, democratic politics and international law. So I am not fully and exhaustively defined as a Jew when I make such criticisms" (Butler, "Response," 394). While I have no issue with Butler's efforts to offer a less unitary self with which to align her positions on Israel, her insistence that her ideas be aligned with a self, however heteronomous, nevertheless remains predicated upon a presumption that Jewishness operates as a form of identity that might be associated with a set of beliefs defined by their particular contents. It is this fundamental alignment of identity and belief, however internally divided the self or the set of ideas in question, that I am arguing fundamentally misconstrues the nature of Jewishness, which is predicated not upon the content of beliefs but upon a subject's willingness to follow established public laws and rituals. As I argue in greater depth below, it is the essential law-centered, public, and collective nature of Jewish practice that complicates any absolute, hard-and-fast distinction between Judaism and Zionism. I say this even as I acknowledge the non-identity of the two modes of collective organization.

one, since it is Butler herself who has selected the writers she engages because of their Jewishness, a Jewishness which, as we have seen, enables her to distinguish anti-Semitism and anti-Zionism. And as the introduction proceeds, Butler does not so much back away from her identitarianism as she relabels it. Suddenly, the identitarianism that would select some resources over others not because of their express content but because of their Jewishness is not Butler's but that of "Zionism." "Even the critique of Zionism, if exclusively Jewish, extends Jewish hegemony for thinking about the region and becomes, in spite of itself, part of what we might call the Zionist effect. Surely any effort that extends Jewish hegemony in the region is part of the Zionist effect whether or not it understands itself as Zionist or anti-Zionist" (*PW*, 3). The outright rejection of Zionist ideology turns out itself to be Zionist if the reason behind one's rejection of Zionism is that it is commanded by one's ethics as a Jew.

We might fairly conclude that a Zionism so capacious as to give equal warrant to Zionist and anti-Zionist arguments is an ideology characterized more by the identities of its purveyors than the content of its arguments. Which is precisely Butler's point. While at first such a Zionism is acknowledged to be a consequence of the exigencies of Butler's own argumentative logic ("If I win the point on these terms…") as the sentence proceeds, the subjunctive mood of the opening is replaced by presumptive neutrality of the present tense of Butler's descriptive voice, ("I establish a Jewish perspective that is non-Zionist, even anti-Zionist at the risk of…"), effectively materializing this "Zionism" as an instantiation of an ever-advancing Israeli colonialism. The subsuming of writerly argument by authorial identity, essential to her project of rendering anti-Zionism and anti-Semitism distinct from one another, becomes, *mirabile dictu,* not Butler's, but Zionism's.

What I have been calling Butler's identitarianism can be seen, moreover, to inflect the modes of rhetorical authority she assumes for herself. It is undoubtedly in the nature of introductions to offer promises about the work to come and thus to move between a present tense in which the reader reads what the author analyzes and a future tense in which the author describes an argument the reader has yet to encounter. But here, tellingly, Butler's predicative aspect of choice is not future, but future perfect — "If I succeed [...], then I will have managed to show" — a strange hybrid of future and past that leaves the moment and process of showing, the argument itself, thoroughly outside her work's mandate. (The construction "there are Jewish resources" works similarly to displace any agent who might do the arguing, as well as any moment in which arguing might take place.)

While we might presume that the displacement of agency enacted by the future perfect operates in some tension with the identitarian authority I have associated with Butler's rhetorical reliance on renaming, the first of the two passages I have been examining allows us to discern a connection between Butler's propensity for relabeling her own argumentative move as "Zionist" and the relocation of historical contingency to some eternally deferred future. The future perfect aspect operates here something like a verbal form in which the "I" who might act or argue in the present or future is displaced by a subject who describes instead, a small-bore version of free indirect discourse. If a simple future tense offers us the vision of a subject whose power to act is predicated on the existence of a future undescribable because it does not yet exist, Butler, using the hinge of the "there are," abruptly transmutes the "future" in question from an analysis that may or may not be adequately argued for by Butler herself into a description of a condition that simply is ("If I succeed in showing that there are Jewish resources for the criticism of state violence, the colonial subjugation of populations, expulsion and dispossession..."). In this temporal formulation, description predominates because what people do or say must follow of necessity from who they are, and that is the case because the moment in which they would have acted has already passed or has not yet arrived.

These two attributes of Butler's rhetorical authority — her tendency both to assert axiomatically by way of description and to displace temporally the moment of action, both of her own analytical process and the historical events she would analyze — are effectively synthesized in the form of the appositional strings by which Butler repeatedly extends her argument's reach. The "critique of state violence" (*PW,* 2) Butler frequently evokes "can be construed as a critique of the Jewish state" or "the movement against political Zionism" (*PW,* 3). While we might imagine vehemently opposing a state's policies at a given moment without concluding that our rejection of those policies must of necessity imply a rejection of that state's legitimating principles of sovereignty, Butler repeatedly links the "critique of state violence" with the "critique of the Jewish state" by way of a string of appositives that effectively turns distinct and — here's the crucial thing — potentially interruptable policies or state actions into inevitably linked behaviors. "State violence, the colonial subjugation of populations, expulsion and dispossession" necessarily imply one another, at once analytically interchangeable states and the linked effects of already present and inevitable causes.

Later, by way of a similar logic to the one by which she had conflated an emphasis on Jewish resources in her argument with Jewish hegemony in the Middle East, Butler suggests that determining the history within which to situate one's analysis ought to *follow from* the state practices one had decided to critique ("And of course, it makes a difference whether one is criticizing the principles of Jewish sovereignty that have characterized political Zionism since 1948 or whether one's criticism is restricted to the occupation as illegal and destructive (and so situating itself in a history that starts with 1967) or whether one is more restrictively criticizing certain military actions in isolation from both Zionism and the occupation, such as the assault on Gaza in 2008–9, which included clear war crimes or the growth of settlements, continuing forms of land confiscation of other kinds, or the policies of the current right-wing regime in Israel. *But in each and every case,* there is a question of whether the criticism can be registered publicly as something other than an attack on the Jews or on Jewishness." (*PW,* 118–19)). Surely there is something disconcerting about the suggestion that the historical events one needs to examine are determined by what one thinks about them, since it suggests that the function of historical narratives is to confirm rather than to discover what one believes. But more disturbing is that this mode of historicization makes explicit the vision implied but not articulated in Butler's strings of appositives. In offering a list of political moments and then treating them as if they are interchangeable ("in each and every case"), Butler's account displaces the contingency of historical events and the possibility of political choice that contingency would undergird, and offers in its place the continuity of the analyzing subject — Butler herself — who would recognize the necessary identity of each of those moments.

Butler might actually be committed to the idea that the state violence, land confiscations, and the expansion of settlements follow inevitably from the founding of the Israeli state, but if she is, she needs to make that case. In the absence of any account of the ways in which the specific qualities of Israeli sovereignty necessitate the brutalities that have come in its wake, Butler's descriptive strings function to instantiate the contiguity of her critical authority. Such authority is not a problem in and of itself, but it becomes one when its uninterruptedness is used to make the equivalence of the various conditions she describes appear historically inevitable rather than rhetorical. These rhetorical equivalences obscure the complicated grapplings of politics. More importantly, they make it impossible to envision a specific moment in which citizens, activists, politicians, or even foreign leaders might intervene to alter and disrupt those brutalities.[12]

---

12 In suggesting that the alignment of Zionism and various stages of authorized and unauthorized state expansion is not self-evident, I do not in any way mean to excuse or offer a cover for the state of Israel's occupation of the West Bank and Gaza in the wake of the 1967 war, or for the various human rights violations for which it was responsible both before the occupation and in the many decades since then. Rather, in drawing attention to this rhetorical slide, I hope to alert us to the ways in which certain of Butler's analytical commitments have the effect of hiding other points of analysis. A number of critics have observed that Butler's interest in discovering relationality within subjectivity has had the effect of privileging synchronic notions of the subject over diachronic. See Vincent Lloyd, "Is Critique Theological?," in *Political Theology* 16, no. 4 (2015): 388–91, at 390–91. Butler's interest in the performance of subjectivity rather than the sustenance of

To be clear on where our points of disagreement lie: I am not disagreeing with Butler's contention that supporters of Israel (particularly right-wing supporters, but that is my qualification, not Butler's) often accuse critics of Israel's policies of anti-Semitism. For some of these supporters some of the time, criticism of Israel can look like anti-Semitism because, in what Seyla Benhabib has called Jews' "continuing paranoia of extinction,"[13] they have taken the lesson of a long history of persecution of the Jews to be that anti-Semitism often starts off looking like something far more innocuous. Within such a world view, one can never been too vigilant. Others level the charge cynically, not because they cannot tell the difference between criticism of specific practices of a specific government of a specific Jewish state and racism directed against Jews as Jews, but because, in the aftermath of the attempted Nazi genocide of the Jews, anti-Semitism has become a particularly unacceptable ideology across the political spectrum.

While the narrowing of discourse produced by the too-quick conflation of anti-Semitism and criticism of Israel's state policies has been a topic of wide discussion in journalistic outlets within the organized American Jewish community,[14] among the most comprehensive and powerful indictment of this politics I've encountered is Israeli director Yoav Shamir's documentary feature *Hashmatza* (Defamation). First broadcast on Israel's state-sponsored Channel 2 in December 2009 after making the rounds of international film festival circuit, Shamir's film turns on the referential ambiguity of "defamation" in contemporary politics surrounding Israel. Shamir interviews not only pillars

political and social relations through time has also led her to emphasize ethics over politics or institution building. See Larisa Reznik, "Melancholic Judaism, Ec-static Ethics, Uncertain Politics," *Political Theology* 16, no. 4 (2015): 382–87.

13 Seyla Benhabib, "Ethics without Normativity and Politics without Historicity: On Judith Butler's *Parting Ways*: Jewishness and the Critique of Zionism," *Constellations* 20, no. 1 (2013): 150–63, at 159.

14 The most comprehensive of these accounts is Peter Beinert's self-consciously polemical *The Crisis of Zionism* (New York: Times Books, 2012).

of organized American Jewish "anti-defamation" politics like
the Anti-Defamation League's Abraham Foxman and Museum
of Tolerance founder Marvin Hier,[15] but US critics of Israel like
Norman Finkelstein, political scientist and author of *The Holocaust Industry: Reflections on the Exploitation of Jewish Suffering*
(2000) and John J. Mearsheimer, co-author of *The Israel Lobby
and US Foreign Policy*, both of whom were targets of charges of
anti-Semitism. So where Butler and I agree both as to the existence of a contemporary discourse conflating criticism of Israel
and anti-Semitism and to the dangers of such political constric-
tion, the frame upon which *Parting Ways* builds its argument
excludes the possibility that Yoav Shamir, a citizen of Israel,
might agree as well, caught as he is within the rhetorical shack-
les of an appositional chain linking Israeli sovereignty to colonial subjugation, expulsion, and dispossession. To clarify: what
is objectionable about the structure of *Parting Ways* is not that
it is predicated on the notion that who is making an argument
or embracing a set of ideas of practices matters to our understanding of that argument or that set of ideas or practices. Both
old and new historicist accounts of literary production rest on
the idea that there is some significant, if not fully determining,
relation between a given writer's historical moment, his or her
positioning, conscious or otherwise, within the multiple forc-
es and frameworks of that moment, and the work that writer
produces. But Butler is arguing something that goes far beyond
historicism. Because Butler makes the case for the separability
of anti-Semitism and anti-Zionism by an identitarian logic that
she then goes on to label "Zionism," Zionists — i.e., citizens of
Israel — aren't simply shaped by their historical location. Rather,
in Butler's account, Zionists are unique in the comprehensive-
ness and capaciousness of their condition of determination:
they can't help but embrace a Zionist (identitarian) ideology

---

15 Wendy Brown offers a subtle reading of the politics of the Museum of Toler-
    ance's central permanent exhibition in *Regulating Aversion: Tolerance in the
    Age of Identity and Empire* (Princeton: Princeton University Press, 2006),
    ch. 5: "Tolerance as Museum Object: The Simon Wiesenthal Center Mu-
    seum of Tolerance."

that holds that all criticisms of Israel are indistinguishable from attacks on Jews. The problem with Butler's argument is that it is predicated on the notion that only certain people can have certain ideas, or, more pointedly, that holding one set of ideas, or, even more disturbingly, being one sort of person, prohibits one from having another set of ideas. Within such a framework, relations of distinction are converted into relations of mutual exclusion.[16]

While Butler's account excludes the possibility of Israeli self-criticism by fiat, simply enumerating counter-examples nevertheless seems to me of limited analytical value. I draw attention to this act of relabeling because I hope to show that the sort of descriptive authority that Butler assumes in the opening pages of her book and that structures the book throughout is fundamentally connected to the model of cultural and intellectual production she both describes and deploys, one in which cultural productions are understood to be significant insofar as they function primarily as modes of self-expression, marks of identity that register the irreducible particularity of their makers. Although we have come to associate the impulse to value objects, ideas, and beliefs for their status as inalienable forms of individual self-expression with what we call "identity politics," I want to suggest that this mode of valuing actually has a much longer and more specific discursive pedigree, one with Locke's "Letter Concerning Toleration" at its origin. This discourse has also come to structure contemporary understandings of secularism, particularly as it is conceived in the United States — that

---

16 Perhaps we are more likely to recognize the importance of the possibility of these sorts of internal critiques when they come under threat. Israeli cultural critic Ariella Azoulay has identified the recent trend in Israel of substituting military operations for declared wars. (This trend is alive in the United States as well, though the US context is outside Azoulay's topic of investigation.) While declared wars require parliamentary debate and authorization, military operations can be conducted from entirely within the military's own structure of command, and thus circumvent the democratic process altogether. See Azoulay, "Declaring the State of Israel: Declaring a State of War," *Critical Inquiry* 37, no. 2 (2011): 265–85.

complex of ideas glossed, however loosely, by the phrase "separation of church and state."[17]

---

17 I've been suggesting that the "identitarian" model of belief undergirding Butler's critique of Zionism borrows its logic from models of Christian belief and the notions of secularism derived from such belief-centric models, and have suggested that such a model might itself be productively analyzed rather than taken as given. In this regard, my essay participates in the body of scholarly work that has come over the past two decades to be known as "post-secularism." Where the notion of secularism articulated by Locke and his 17th-century contemporaries made the case that governments might disengage from the regulation of religion because "religion" was a set of states of private conscience structuring individual believers' relations to a deity, post-secularists including Talal Asad, Saba Mahmood, and Charles Taylor have historicized the achievement of this belief-centered model so as to allow us to see it as something other than what Taylor terms a "subtraction story," a straightforward negation or privatization of religion. In Taylor's *A Secular Age* (Cambridge: Harvard University Press, 2007), secularism is indeed a phenomenon particular to "Latin Christianity." Developments within Christianity — the narrowing of the gap between spiritual practices expected of religious elites and laypeople; the emergence of measures of purity and discipline; the shift in emphasis from embodied practices to "a set of beliefs in a set of propositions" (16) — transformed religion from the horizon of existence into an intertwined set of beliefs and practices, not primarily as a transcending of delusion but as a condition in which belief is made optional. For scholars like Asad and Mahmood, the changes within Taylor identifies within Latin Christianity were not simply internal to it but were generated by its encounter "with numerous other religious traditions in the course of its missionary and colonizing projects across Latin America, Australia, Africa, Asia, and the Middle East" (Saba Mahmood, "Can Secularism Be Other-wise?" in *Varieties of Secularism in a Secular Age,* eds. Michael Warner, Jonathan Vanantwerpen, and Craig Calhoun [Cambridge: Harvard University Press, 2010], 285). To tell this story of secularism as a story of Christianity alone is to fail to account for the ways in which, to take just one example, "the emphasis on personal conversion, witnessing and close fellowship were sharpened and defined through missionary work, the responsibility ordinary Europeans came to feel to bring the gospel to 'heathens' and those living in ignorance of Christ's truth" (287). But in Mahmood's critique of Taylor, like mine of Butler, the characterization of secularism's genealogy as an autonomously Western, Christian movement is symptomatic of longstanding dynamics both internal to Christianity itself and to the history of writing about Christianity. For both Christians and a range of Enlightenment writers who took the topic as their focus, what made Christianity something other than one among many religious

forms was its singular capacity to rise above its historicity, its cultural and doctrinal particularity to embody universalist principles.

What Taylor's genealogy of secularism and Asad and Mahmood's post-colonial critique of that genealogy do not provide is a framework for understanding the particular history of the relation of Jewish spiritual practices or collective life to the European nation-state. Because the shifting combinations of legal forms, collective ceremonial practices, and propositional beliefs that constituted "Jewishness" preexisted Christianity and in many ways provided the framework against which Christianity defined itself, Jewishness stands in its various forms and combinations in notably different relation to the history of a Christianity that mutated into secularism by way of some complex dynamic of internally generated purification and spiritualization and the encounter with colonial subjects than the spiritual practices of those colonial subjects do.

And to the degree Jewish "practice" was law-based and public, as much civil as theological, the "Jewish people" can be seen to have occupied a complex relation to the history of the modern nation-state as well. The date most frequently identified as the initiating moment of the European colonial enterprise — 1492 — is also, and not coincidentally, the year in which the Jewish population of Spain was legally expelled from Spanish territory. As Jonathan Scheer's detailed history of the colonial dismantling of the Ottoman Empire makes apparent, even if we turn to more recent and geographically proximate history, we have difficulty unambiguously aligning either the anti-Zionist Jews whom Butler retrospectively celebrates or the members of the Zionist Federation of Great Britain and Ireland who in 1917 received notice that "His Majesty's government view with favor the establishment in Palestine of a national home for the Jewish people" with European colonial authority. The British Zionists were recipients of, rather than signatories to the letter known as the Balfour Declaration, which went on — in the very same sentence — to insist that "it be [...] clearly understood that nothing shall be done which may prejudice the civil and religious rights of existing non-Jewish communities in Palestine, or the rights and political status enjoyed by Jews in any other country." Given that the British had, only two years earlier, struck a secret pact with the French known as the Sykes–Picot agreement dividing most of the Arab territories of the former Ottoman Empire between the British and the French and placing Palestine itself under international administration, the Declaration seemed motivated by the British desire to rewrite the terms of that agreement so as to engage international support for unilateral British control of Palestine in the name of establishing a Jewish homeland. In the decades that followed, the British Prime Minister Churchill would issue a "White Paper" that suggested that both Arab and Jewish inhabitants of Palestine were to be considered "Palestinian"; the Peel Commission would, in 1937, offer a revised proposal that placed only fifteen percent of Mandatory Palestine under Jewish control (the bulk of the territory was to be split between an Arab state and

I turn now to Locke's letter with the object of recovering a brief and select history of the emergence of belief as a structure for managing the limitations of agency and knowledge in a con-

---

a not-fully defined international zone); and, finally, the MacDonald White Paper would declare, in May 1939, that it was "not part of the British government's policy that Palestine should become a Jewish state," and would radically limit Jewish immigration to Palestine accordingly. The British would also, in response to a cluster of military setbacks during World War I, pursue a series of agreements designed to broker peace with the Turks by leaving the Middle East under Ottoman control, which had they been accepted by Turkish officials, would have effectively canceled the pledges of political autonomy made both to the region's Arabs and to its Jews. Nor is it self-evident — and here we venture into the tricky theoretical terrain of counter-history — that the 1947 UN Partition Declaration that formally divided the territory held under the British Mandate into Jewish and Arab national homelands would have gained the international support necessary for its passage by the General Assembly if the Jewish communities of Europe had not been devastated by the Nazi genocide directed against them. So while *Parting Ways* takes as axiomatic political Zionism's status as "settler colonialism" (16), once we actually examine the circuitous and altogether unpredictable set of events by which the early Zionists of the Yishuv came to control the territory that became 1948 Israel, we are likely to find ourselves hard-pressed to make the case that either Yishuv leaders or Jewish advocates of Zionism living elsewhere functioned or were understood to be the emissaries of a broader European colonial project.

In making the case that neither the history of Jews nor the history of Zionism can be straightforwardly accommodated within the paradigm of colonial encounter that undergirds either Taylor's history or Mahmood's and Asad's respective counter-histories, I'm not suggesting that the current Israeli occupation of the West Bank, and the circumscription of the lives of the West Bank's Palestinian residents by various forms of military discipline and direct and indirect commercial and social disruption is anything besides a morally indefensible and politically unsustainable colonial regime. I am suggesting, however, that the fact that, throughout the period of European colonial consolidation and expansion stretching from the 15th to the early 20th century, Jews not only were not identified with the political apparatus of any European nation-state, but were often subject to arbitrary exercises of that authority, including frequent expulsions, means that the establishment of a "national home for the Jewish people" in the aftermath of the dissolution of the British mandate and the withdrawal of the French and British colonial presence in the Middle East need not be understood as a colonial enterprise in itself. See Mahmood, "Can Secularism Be Otherwise?"; Jonathan Scheer, *The Balfour Declaration: The Origins of the Arab-Israeli Conflict* (New York: Random House, 2010).

tingent material world, along with an account of the constraints of such a solution. But my goal in introducing this broader historical trajectory is not merely to suggest that the logic of identity politics Butler invokes, however uncharacteristically, has its origins in a Lockean conception of belief and toleration. To understand why it is that Locke conceives belief to be the perfect form of self-expression, the ideal instantiation of identity, and why he values such an instantiation, we need to read his "Letter on Toleration" in the context of his foundational work on liberalism and private property. As we shall see, Locke understands the immateriality of belief to be a solution to constraints imposed by material scarcity, constraints he otherwise looks to governments to manage, if not solve entirely. Insofar as such a conception of belief promises an immediate solution to the problems of sustaining a self in the world without the intervention of political institutions, Locke's writing allows us to see that Butler's fantasy of a believing subject whose ethical relations to itself and to others dispense with the need for political institutions is a fantasy with a very long historical pedigree.

∾∾∾

IN THE CANONICAL HISTORY OF WESTERN political thought, the place of Locke's *Second Treatise of Government* is well established.[18] While Locke's early modern predecessor Thomas Hobbes saw the state, undergirded by the authority of an absolute monarch, as a necessary precondition for any sort of sustained,

---

18 The relevant scholarly literature is vast, much too large to offer an accounting of here. C.B. Macpherson's *The Political Theory of Possessive Individualism* (Oxford: Oxford University Press, 1962) has long been seen as offering the canonical reading of Locke as a progenitor of modern liberalism. Some works especially relevant to my thinking here are Kirstie McClure, *Judging Rights: Lockean Politics and the Limits of Consent* (Ithaca: Cornell University Press, 1996); and Jeremy Waldron, *God, Locke and Equality: Foundations of Locke's Political Thought* (Cambridge: Cambridge University Press, 2002).

non-violent sociability, Locke famously envisioned a much more limited role for the state. Earlier thinkers had viewed private property as something like a gift from a (sometimes divinely ordained) king to his subjects. For Locke, by contrast, individuals' right to property preexisted the state, and in that sense deserved to be protected from any unwarranted appropriation by the king. In what is perhaps the Second Treatise's most well-known passage, Locke lays out the grounds for individuals' right to property:

> Though the Earth, and all inferior Creatures be common to all Men, yet every Man has a *Property* in his own *Person*. This no Body has any Right to but himself. The *Labour* of his Body, and the *Work* of his Hands, we may say, are properly his. Whatsoever then he removed out of the State that Nature hath provided, and left it in, he hath mixed his *Labour* with, and joined to it something that is his own, and thereby makes it his *Property*. It being by him removed from the common state Nature placed it in, it hath by this *Labour* something annexed to it, that excludes the common right of other Men. For this *Labour* being the unquestionable Property of the Labourer, no Man but he can have a right to what that is once joined to, at least where there is enough, and as good left in common for others.[19]

The right to private property, as Locke explains it, follows from the individual's exclusive — and inalienable — right to his own body. The material world begins as an undifferentiated mass granted by God to the human race in common, but the very fact that the world has been allocated *in common* prevents any particular individual from making use of any element of the material world without effectively infringing upon the rights of the other people who constitute the common. Locke understands the solution to this conundrum to lie in the capacity of the la-

---

19 John Locke, *Two Treatises of Government,* ed. Peter Laslett (Cambridge: Cambridge University Press, 1988), 287–88.

bor of individuals to remake and transmute the material world. Because individuals have the exclusive right to their own bodies, when they combine those bodies with the material world by working the stuff of that world, those individuals gain an exclusive right to that stuff they have remade. In this account, property is fundamentally a kind of individual *self-expression,* a transformation of the material world by way of labor particular to and identifying of one individual and not another. Having alienated their inalienable bodies, Lockean individuals possess the exclusive right to reclaim what they have sent away, by virtue of having sent it away. I mean for the paradoxical quality of Locke's vision to be apparent in my paraphrase. The inalienable right to one's own body can only be made manifest by way of its "alienation" in the form of labor, but once those bodies and the property they bring into being are alienated, there is nothing — natural rights notwithstanding — to assure that they will not be appropriated by someone else. Nothing, that is, until Locke, several passages on into his argument, imagines a government brought into being precisely for the role of keeping people's property their own, of assuring that the alienated self-expressions are returned to their proper owners.

I offer this rehearsal of Locke's labor theory of value not because there is anything especially original about my parsing — there isn't — but because it offers a crucial framework for understanding what is at stake in Locke's formulation of the nature of belief and the proper relation of the state to that belief. The "Letter Concerning Toleration" (1689), when all is said and done, is a meditation on the nature of state power, its analysis of belief drafted to the cause of delineating the civil sphere's limit case. That is, Locke offers an analogy between the forms of self-expression instantiated in the material realm — property — and those forms of expression instantiated in the eternal, immaterial realm — belief — in order to make clear what government ought and ought not be given the power to regulate. The business of civil government, Locke writes, is "by the impartial execution of equal laws, to secure unto all the people in general, and to every one of [the] subjects in particular the just possession of these things belonging to this life."[20]The role of the government is to make sure material property stays with its proper owners. Beyond that work of making the alienated expression inalienable, there is nothing left for government to do:

> Every man has an immortal soul, capable of eternal happiness or misery; whose happiness depending upon his believing and doing those things in this life which are necessary to the obtaining of God's favour, and are prescribed by God to that end. It follows from thence, first, that the observance of these things is the highest obligation that lies upon mankind, and that our utmost care, application, and diligence ought to be exercised in the search and performance of them; because there is nothing in this world that is of any consideration in comparison with eternity. [...]
>
> But besides their souls, which are immortal, men have also their temporal lives here upon earth; the state whereof being frail and fleeting, and the duration uncertain, they have need of several outward conveniences to the support thereof, which are to be procured or preserved by pains and industry. For those things that are necessary to the comfortable support of our lives are not the spontaneous products of nature, nor do offer themselves fit and prepared for our use. This part therefore draws on another care, and necessarily gives another employment. ("L," 241–42)

While Locke begins by emphasizing the analogy between the temporal and eternal realms, as his argument unfolds, it is the *differences* between the two realms that become most salient. As the essay proceeds, what becomes clear is the extent to which government authority is justified as an instrument of *compensation,* a means of making the political subject more like the immortal subject. The government comes into being in order to

---

20 John Locke , "Letter Concerning Toleration" (1689), in *Two Treatises of Government and A Letter Concerning Toleration* (New Haven: Yale University Press, 2003), 172. Henceforth, "L."

adjudicate among individuals' competing property claims — different versions of deviation from the common — which it does by establishing a point of view independent of any identified by the competing individuals. The state, in this account, is not quite something that all its citizens generate in common. Instead, it operates in the gap created by the impossibility of stably and permanently establishing such value.

So if Locke understands private property to be first and foremost a kind of individual self-expression, in the "Letter," belief, or faith, is revealed to be an especially valuable form of self-expression for one crucial reason: it is a kind of property that cannot be stolen. Faith is distinguished from willed industry and the property that manifests such industry (and removes it from temporality) by its non-fungibility.

> [T]he pravity of mankind being such that they had rather injuriously prey upon the fruits of other men's labours than take pains to provide for themselves, the necessity of preserving men in the possession of what honest industry has already acquired, and also of preserving their liberty and strength, whereby they may acquire what they rather want, obliges men to enter into society with one another, that by mutual assistance and joint force they may secure unto each other their properties, in the things that contribute to the comfort and happiness of this life, leaving in the meanwhile to every man the care of his own eternal happiness, the attainment whereof can neither be facilitated by another man's industry, nor can the loss of it turn to another man's prejudice, nor the hope of it be forced from him by any external violence. ("L," 242)

In this account, belief can safely be left outside the realm of government power in part because such power is unnecessary to keep beliefs attached to their believers — to keep their self-expressions, their property, as their own. Insofar as it does not require this additional institutional force to shore it up, belief both marks and produces the absolute individuality of its subject. The religious subject's freedom from state control is at once presumed, presented as an inherent value, and argued for. The rhetorical effect of the passage's sequence is to suggest that the value of faith as a category lies in its resistance as a form of expression to being appropriated by others. But belief stands as the ideal expression of the subject in an even more fundamental way: it does not presuppose the existence of a common culture, a more generally accepted set of social values, for its meaning and significance. Belief is eternal rather than temporal not simply because the object of its attention — God — is itself eternal, but because its meaning exists independent of historically local societies of values.

In order to grasp the full import of Locke's argument about toleration, we need to consider the role that his claim for the autonomy of belief plays within his larger system of economic, political, institutional, and social relations. Where Locke's insistence on the analogy between the realms of belief and property reveals the "pravity," the imperfection, of the temporal realm in all its property-centered sociability, his assertion of the two realms' likeness also serves as a means of justifying governmental authority. The role of the civil government thus becomes to exercise its policing, judiciary function so as to approximate in the civil realm the non-appropriability of identity that distinguishes the realm of faith. The operation of civil law is successful insofar as it prevents one political subject from appropriating the industry or expression — that is to say, the property — of someone else. Such politics can never achieve its end: politics and belief, after all, have absolutely different relations to time, and there is no assurance that the fact of having secured property to its owner up until a given moment will guarantee its security in perpetuity. In the temporal world of history and accident, there's always time for something to go amiss. But for Locke, the elusiveness of politics' end becomes proof of its necessary validity. The fact that the condition of absolute non-fungibility that is constitutive of belief does not and cannot exist within the temporal realm is precisely what defines belief's value. By this account, moreover, both property and belief matter because they are modes of self-expression. That the former can stand in for the latter becomes the evidence of their likeness to one another, and such analogy in turn testifies to the purely formal status of their expressiveness. Property and belief are like one another, that is, only so long as what matters about them is that they are expressed by a given subject, such that the particular content of a given belief and the particular qualities of a given parcel of property are entirely beside the point.

It is this uniqueness of belief implicit in its quality of non-appropriability that effectively undergirds Butler's argument for the mutual exclusiveness of anti-Semitism and anti-Zionism (or of Judaism and Zionism). Only so long as an individual's beliefs are understood to correlate exactly and exclusively with that individual can a description of identity ("Jewish (resources)") function in and of itself as evidence of a necessary limit on the range of beliefs that can be held. (This particular position critical of Israel cannot be anti-Jewish because it is expressed by Jews (found in "Jewish resources").) But what Locke's formulation also allows us to see is that the claim that a belief is autonomous from the state by virtue of its status as the unique expression of an individual subject not only stands as evidence of that subject's interpellation within the state, but also actually serves to undergird and justify an authority external to that subject — here, the authority of the state. If the singularity of an individual's expression not only lends that expression its value and keeps it from being appropriated by someone else, but also authorizes the exercise of whatever external authority is necessary to keep expression and expressor linked, then how does this dual logic play itself out within Butler's argument? Following Locke through a final, not wholly anticipatable, swerve in his argument can provide us with a framework for making sense of some of the syntactic tics in Butler's rhetoric that earlier appeared merely idiosyncratic.

Locke's emphasis on the structural symmetry of the temporal and eternal realms would seem to undergird a purely formal understanding of belief. Once he attempts to account for the fates of individual subjects, however, his notion of belief, as well as of the relation between faith and private property, is transformed in some remarkable ways. Having just made the case for the general — that is to say, formal — invulnerability of inward states of consciousness to the sorts of external coercion wielded by civil authorities — one's beliefs, unlike one's things, cannot be stolen — Locke offers a final rationale for the cordoning off of the realm of belief from the pressures of the civil realm:

> In the third place, the care of the salvation of men's souls cannot belong to the magistrate; because, though the rigour of laws and the force of penalties were capable to convince and change men's minds, yet would not that help at all to the salvation of their souls. For there being but one truth, one way to heaven, what hope is there that more men would be led into it if they had no rule but the religion of their own consciences, and blindly to resign themselves up to the will of their governors and to the religion which either ignorance, ambition, or superstition had chanced to establish in the countries where they were born? In the variety and contradiction of opinions in religion, wherein the princes of the world are as much divided as in their secular interests, the narrow way would be much straitened; one country alone would be in the right, and all the rest of the world put under and obligation of following their princes in the ways that lead to destruction; and that which heightens the absurdity, and very ill suits the notion of a Deity, men would owe their eternal happiness or misery to the places of their nativity. ("L," 220)

With a sudden shifting of rhetorical gears, Locke here opts to half-withdraw the formal case he has made for keeping the religious and civil realms distinct so as to make an argument for the particular quality of religious faith. Where elsewhere, he painstakingly argued for the non-appropriability or non-fungibility attendant upon states of consciousness per se, suddenly he is willing to concede the possibility that "the rigour of laws and the force of penalties [might be] capable [of] convinc[ing] or chang[ing] men's minds." Earlier, Locke insisted there was no reason for the government to interfere with the beliefs of its citizens because no government influence could alter a belief that arose immutably from the singular consciousness of the believer, and which was significant as a consequence of that singular and immutable origin. Suddenly, Locke acknowledges governments can indeed force their citizens to adopt beliefs that they otherwise might not be willing to sign onto, but the efficacy of such government coercion becomes the reason it must not be allowed. If the threat of civil penalties might indeed succeed in convincing individuals to change what it is they believe, nonetheless, such civil persuasion "would not [...] help at all to the salvation of their souls," given that such governmentally coerced beliefs might in fact be wrong, and would thus operate to direct their possessors away from "the one way to heaven." Possessing the sort of faith that eventuates in the salvation of one's soul is no longer simply the state of conviction it appeared to be at the beginning of Locke's account, the sort of "inward persuasion of the mind" that remains inalienably one's own by definition, by virtue of being constituted by one's own subjective state. Instead, salvation turns out to rest on having the correct conviction — the "one truth, one way to heaven." Certain beliefs are true, however one has arrived at them; others are untrue. Given this reconfiguration, the case for toleration is not to be made on formal grounds — people must have unconstrained right to their beliefs because their beliefs are theirs — but on the grounds of the singularity of true belief — people must have the right to believe in the one true faith without being constrained by the misbegotten sectarian commitments of the rulers of their native countries. How unfair it would be for some citizens to be denied access to the one true way and the eternal salvation just because they've had the bad luck to be born and educated in countries led by wrong-headed sovereigns!

I want to suggest that Locke's decision to advance both a formal rationale for tolerance and at the same time a rationale based on the singularity of true belief marks neither an analytical lapse nor a kind of covering-all-bases eclecticism. Rather, we ought to see his divided case for the free exercise of faith to be part of his effort to describe what he understands to be the peculiarly doubled, delicately not-quite-paradoxical nature of Christian faith to be. It is faith's capacity to be both belief in something — an objective condition that might be recognized by others — and belief unanchored and unmodified — a state of consciousness that matters because it marks and names one's own ineffable and inalienable consciousness — that compels Locke. And it is in relation to this dual quality of belief that his labor theory of value comes to stand as not simply a description of the fallenness of the material world, the world of made things, but as the most perfect expression of that belief, an ineffably particular condition of consciousness made real for all to see.[21]

---

21 While Locke's "Letter" is not an explicit object of analysis, the philosopher Akeel Bilgrami has recently offered a provocative history of the period that helps make sense of the particular qualities of the incoherence of Locke's case for toleration. In Bilgrami's account, the motivations for what he calls, following Taylor, "the forced inaccessibility of God" were as much economic and political as they were epistemological or spiritual. When a furious debate erupted within the British scientific establishment toward the end of the 17th century over whether the newly hegemonic Newtonian laws of physics need imply a vision of the natural world in which God was absent from its ongoing operations, establishment members of the Royal Society ultimately triumphed over dissenters like John Toland not because Newton's vision necessarily invalidated the sort of Spinoza-influenced pantheism that understood God to be present in nature and providing an internal sense of dynamism, but because the Royal Society ideologues forged an alliance with emergent commercial and mercantile interests. Once God was no longer understood to be everywhere in nature, then nature became available as a *resource,* something available to be mined, transformed into plantation agriculture, deforested. In the political realm, the notion of a "God present in all things and all bodies" (the phrase is the Leveller Gerrard Winstanley's) invited a democratization of access to both God and other forms of authority that threatened the exclusive authority of the Protestant religious elite: "The form of cognitive elitism bestowed by this metaphysics on an Anglican priestcraft was generalized to a cognitive elitism much more broadly in matters of law and political governance." Bilgrami concludes: "The broad analogy [was] that a monarch and his courtly entourage of propertied elites ruling over a brute populace was just a mundane version of the ideal of an external [i.e., functionally absent] God ruling over a brute universe" (*Secularism, Identity, and Enchantment* [Cambridge: Harvard University Press, 2014], 189).

While Locke makes no effort to acknowledge, much less to resolve, this contradiction within his description of the nature of belief, this incoherence at the heart of his "Letter Concerning Toleration" nonetheless offers a revealing analytical framework through which to analyze the implications of the peculiar structure of *Parting Ways*. As we saw in Locke, the mutual reflection of identity and belief articulates a vision in which the irreducible uniqueness of the individual and his or her belief possess the power to render the force of the material and historical worlds outside the individual, including any and all relations to

---

In these overlapping debates, then, we find the two positions articulated and yet left unreconciled in Locke's "Letter": first, the radically "democratic" position that individuals' beliefs are worthy of protection because they are theirs; and, second, the position that individuals' freedom of belief must be protected because no competing institutions, be they political or religious, ought to have the authority to inhibit individuals' access to the one, true belief. But Bilgrami's essay is instructive for understanding the logic and limitations of Locke's argument in other ways as well, ways in which Bilgrami himself seems less fully in control. Having ventured a historical context by which to make sense of "the exile [of God] into inaccessibility from the visions of ordinary people to a place outside the universe" (ibid., 147), Bilgrami abruptly shifts disciplinary and rhetorical modes, abandoning historicism for philosophy in order to make the case for the "reenchantment" of the world. Where pages earlier individual agency had seemed something that might be diffused or consolidated by the opportunistic confederation of natural philosophers and mercantile capitalists, suddenly agency becomes an ontology. "There can be no notion of agency," Bilgrami announces, "when one has a conception of value as residing entirely in our desires and moral sentiments rather than as external callings that make demands on us, to which our desires and moral sentiments are responses" (ibid., 153). If an unholy alliance of science and capital has brought us to the disenchanted universe we now inhabit, for Bilgrami, this disenchantment is to be mourned not because it is historically contingent or politically or ethically unsavory, but because it makes no sense philosophically. We need to reintroduce a notion of value beyond the human because only so long as there is a source of value external yet accessible to humans — the sort of animating power envisioned by Toland and his band of Spinoza-inspired pantheists — can humans be agents, rather than "mere receptacles for our desires and their satisfactions" (ibid., 155). With this shift to the philosophical, Bilgrami replicates rather than analyzes the movement of Locke's "Letter," as the subject who can escape historical marking comes to justify the aspirations of the subject who cannot.

the state, entirely inconsequential. Locke's second movement, in which the non-interference of the state is designed to ensure that individuals are not blocked from the one true truth by the historical accident of their birth, marks the return of the authority of a singular truth, and with it, an insistence upon the realness of a shared world. But insofar as the authority determining that truth lies entirely beyond the human realm, the truth of the world is asserted rather than discovered or negotiated. In both these aspects, Locke's — and Butler's — worlds of belief are worlds without politics. In the first aspect, in which belief is a form of self-expression, this is because everyone and everything outside the unique belief of a unique individual is beside the point and thus not worth negotiating. There can be no scarcity in a world in which things cannot be passed from one person to the next, in which nothing can be shared. In a world without scarcity, a government justified in terms of its authority to adjudicate among competing claims to the same material objects quite literally has nothing to do. In the second aspect, in which belief marks a singular truth, the transcendent truth of Jesus Christ, there can be no politics because the truth of the shared world has already been determined elsewhere, beyond the realm of the tug and counter-tug of competing interests and values.[22]

---

22 In her essay, "A Diasporic Critique of Diasporism: The Question of Jewish Political Agency," *Political Theory* 43, no. 1 (2015): 80–110, Julie E. Cooper takes Butler to task for *Parting Ways*'s celebration of a diasporic ethics of "self-departure" or "dispossession," — conditions of selfhood — at the expense of an engagement with the questions of self-determination and political agency that Zionism came into being to address. "Butler's ethical turn is predicated on a misdiagnosis," Cooper argues. [Zionist founder Theodor] Herzl's investment in the state does not betray "identitarian commitments" — for Herzl defines Jewish nationality as "the contingent product of persecution" (19). Cooper: "In Butler's argument, the contingencies of Jewish history (e.g. the Holocaust) provide occasion for the derivation of 'principles of justice and equality and respect for life and land.' By deriving such a framework Butler hopes to advance concrete political goals, including the critique of the nation-state. To derive generalizable ethical principles (applicable to Jews) is not, however, to examine how this dispersed people can exercise political agency and confront political challenges. [...]

We find the echo of this second world governed by a singular truth not in the models of subjectivity Butler envisions as the goal of her critique, but rather in the rhetoric she employs to advance it. Earlier I noted the way in which Butler toggles between a future-directed subjunctive and a strangely already-completed future perfect in order to describe an argument that is done without ever having been made ("*If* I succeed [...], I *will* have *managed* to show"). But were this self-affirming authority merely confined to the rhetorical structure of Butler's argument, we might reasonably chalk up the slide from potential to already done as a moment of argumentative imprecision, the promising over-promising to which introductions often fall victim. With the appositional string Butler introduces immediately after, however, in which a range of historical moments spanning decades and a range of possible attitudes toward those historical moments are named and then immediately conflated with one another ("in each and every case"), Butler extends her authority from the rhetorical relations operative within her own argument to the links among historical events. With this redescription, it is not simply Butler's argument but history itself that is finished before it has begun, with the contingency of history admitted only to be rendered inevitable, one true way to heaven (or hell). If the authority of *Parting Ways*'s "Jewish resources" lies in their capacity fully to define by the mere fact of their writers' identities the force of the positions articulated within them, Butler's authority matters not because it is hers but because it functions like Locke's Christian form of divine power, endowed with the capacity to turn the interruptable swerves and hiccups of history into one inescapable-because-already-finished outcome. Butler's authority is neither confined to the realm of her own rhetoric nor located within historical time, and in this regard constitutes itself as both singular and non-contingent, an authority that creates relations of cause-and-effect within the

---

The proper object of diasporic critique [...] is not solidarity, belonging or communitarianism, but the poverty of political imagination when it comes to envisioning political agency beyond the nation-state" (ibid., 21–22).

world without being quite of that world. Like the singular truth of Locke's "one true path," Butler's voice renders historical events separated by decades inevitable consequences of one another, impervious to the disruptions of politics or distraction, and, in so doing, makes politics both impossible and unnecessary.

∾∾∾

When, in 1783, Moses Mendelssohn placed Locke's "Letter Concerning Toleration" at the center of his own engagement with the question of religious liberty, his critique of Locke attempted not to make the case for government constraint but instead to place the case for religious liberty on new footing. In arguing for a version of religious liberty capacious enough to encompass models of religiosity more heterogeneous than Locke's one true belief, Mendelssohn does not merely embrace his predecessor's defense of freedom of individual consciousness and expression while jettisoning that defense's link to the authority of exclusive truth. Rather than arguing, as Locke did, for a toleration based on the irrelevance of the state to matters of individual conscience, Mendelssohn lays out an alternative conception of what counts as religious practice and insists that the grounds for the freedom of such practices ought to lie in their continuity with, rather than their distance from, the activities of the state.

Separated by more than a century from Locke's "Letter," *Jerusalem* is not primarily animated by a desire to refute Locke's text. Rather, *Jerusalem* stands as Mendelssohn's attempt to yoke together Locke's argument for limiting civil authority over religious expression and his own analysis of Judaism's departures from what he understands to be the fundamentally Christian Lockean secularist logic, in order to respond to a challenge posed to him by a Berlin contemporary, the Enlightenment writer August Friedrich Cranz. The previous year, Cranz had published a 47-page pamphlet entitled, *The Searching for Light and Right in a Letter to Mr. Moses Mendelssohn Occasioned by his*

TUCKER

*Remarkable Preface to Menasseh ben Israel (Das Forschen nach
Licht und Recht in einem Schreiben an Herrn Moses Mendelssohn
auf Veranlassung seiner merkwurdigen Borrede zu Manasseh
Ben Israel)*, which challenged Mendelssohn to explain why the
statutory ecclesiastical laws of Judaism, including the right to
excommunicate heretics, which not only distinguished Judaism
from Christianity but Jewish civil life from that of other nations
on earth, ought not to be understood as a version of treason.
Cranz, writing anonymously while expressing his admiration
for Mendelssohn throughout, urged Mendelssohn to convert to
Christianity in accordance with the Paulian mandate that understood the Christian spirit as a fulfillment of the Jewish law,
"purified of the onerous statutes of the rabbis augmented by new
elements,"[23] or to explain why he would not. (Mendelssohn had
responded evasively to a similar inquiry by Swiss clergyman
Johann Kasper Lavater more than a decade earlier, affirming
his own loyalty both to German law and to Jewish ecclesiastical practice without directly addressing the possibility of any
contradictions between them.) As for the Remarkable Preface
to Menasseh Ben Israel to which Cranz alludes in his title: in
1782, Mendelssohn had offered a re-edition, in German translation with a new preface of his own, of a treatise by seventeenth-
century Amsterdam rabbi–philosopher Menasseh Ben Israel,
who had made a case for readmitting the Jews to England by
offering a detailed theological argument for the ways in which
Jewish theological authority need not be in tension with the authority of civil society. Mendelssohn had been moved to issue
this new edition of Ben Israel's work not by an attack on the
Jewish right to civil emancipation, but rather by a ringing and
public endorsement of that right. The previous year, Berlin intellectual Christian Wilhelm Dohm had published *On the Civil
Improvement of the Jews,* in which Dohm argued that any "Jew-

---

23 August Friedrich Cranz, *Das Forschen nach Licht und Recht in einem Screi-
ben an Herrn moses Mendelssohn auf Veranlassung seiner merkwurdigen
Vorrede zu Manasseh Ben Israel,* quoted in Alexander Altmann's Introduction to Moses Mendelssohn, *Jerusalem, or On Religious Power and Judaism*
(Hanover: Brandeis University Press, 1983), 9.

ish colony," established within the secular state ought to retain the right to excommunicate Jews who did not adequately conform to its tenets. Mendelssohn disagreed with Dohm's position that the power of excommunication was essential to the nature of Jewish religious authority, and presented Ben Israel's treatise, along with his own prefatory framing of that treatise, as a means of intervening in the very public debate that erupted in the wake of the publication of Dohm's work.[24]

Given such a politically and intellectually complex compositional context, the argument Mendelssohn puts forth in *Jerusalem* shows remarkable theoretical coherence. This coherence has not always been registered in the critical literature, which has tended to understand Mendelssohn's theorization of Jewish religious authority as originating fundamentally from within a semiotic, deontological framework associated most prominently with Kantian thought. While, as we shall see, Mendelssohn does ultimately make the case for a vision of Jewish communal practice organized around a "ritual law" legible within semiotic terms, the force of this semiotic practice is best understood as an attempt to reorganize the terms laid out in Locke's "Letter" so as to support a case for Jewish communal authority without embracing the Dohmian power of excommunication.

Mendelssohn begins by drawing a distinction between "action" and "conviction" — i.e., belief — that would appear to echo Locke's differentiation of labor's fungible objects and the non-fungible objects of belief, only immediately to broaden the terms of the difference. Mendelssohn announces: "Action accomplishes what duty demands, and conviction causes that action to proceed from the proper source, that is, from proper motives."[25] While we might expect this distinction to undergird,

---

24 My account of the intellectual and political context of *Jerusalem's* publication has been drawn from Alexander Altmann's introduction, as well as Leora Batnitzky's *How Judaism Became a Religion* (Princeton University Press, 2011) and Gideon Freudenthal, *No Religion without Idolatry: Mendelssohn's Jewish Enlightenment* (Notre Dame: University of Notre Dame Press, 2012).

25 Mendelssohn, *Jerusalem,* 40. Henceforth, *J.*

as it did for Locke, the distinction between the fungible sorts of self-expression that governments might regulate and those non-fungible beliefs that must by definition remain beyond the reach of institutional regulation, Mendelssohn in fact refuses these now-familiar taxonomical alignments. What Locke acknowledged only grudgingly and in contradiction with the central principles of much of his argument — that governmental authority, employed explicitly via institutions and more indirectly by way of pressure upon social norms, can affect individual citizens' beliefs — functions for Mendelssohn as a point of departure. In Mendelssohn's view, both individuals' actions and their convictions can be directed by "public institutions," with people moved to actions by "reasons that motivate the will" and to convictions by "reasons that persuade by their truth," i.e., "education." Mendelssohn's focus on the motivations directing what we might call the disposition of subjectivity, rather than the material forms into which such modes of subjectivity are translated, is crucial. To understand what he is up to, we need first to recognize what his account of culture is not: it is not a notion of culture predicated upon a labor theory of value, which is to say, it is not a version of culture in which states of consciousness become common, become culture, by being translated into a shareable made world. For Mendelssohn, the significance of an action, event or made thing in the world has little to do with its purity as a translation or expression of an inner state of consciousness.

> The man who avoids deception because he loves honesty is happier than one who is merely afraid of the arbitrary punishments of the state linked with fraud. But to his fellow man, it does not matter what motives cause the wrong to remain undone, or by what means his rights and property are safeguarded. (J, 44)

Where Locke began by insisting that belief be understood as a perfect form of the individual self-expression imperfectly manifested as labor and private property, and saw the perfection of belief as leaving government with nothing to regulate, for Mendelssohn, it is not possible to know for sure what sort of, if any, link exists between internal states of conviction and externally legible actions. Because the link cannot be known, religious authorities ought not to be empowered to regulate the beliefs of their adherents by way of excommunication. What matters — what ought to matter — is how people act, not what sort of thinking motivates their actions.

Mendelssohn thus recharacterizes the conviction/action dyad as a range of motivations producing a variety of outcomes, rather than as a hierarchy of more or less perfect materializations of internal states of consciousness. We can understand the force of Mendelssohn's recharacterization by considering how it follows from his rejection of Locke's fundamental premise of the singularity and uniqueness of eternal life. Early on in *Jerusalem*, Mendelssohn insists that "man's eternality is merely an incessant temporality" (*J*, 39).[26] Mendelssohn elaborates:

> It is [...] neither in keeping with the truth nor advantageous to man's welfare to sever the temporal so neatly from the eternal. At bottom, man will never partake of eternity; his eternality is merely an incessant temporality. His temporality never ends; it is, therefore, an essential part of his permanency and inseparable from it. One confuses ideas if one opposes his temporal welfare to his eternal felicity. (*J*, 39)

By Mendelssohn's account, the transcendence of the individual takes place not by way of its limitlessness but by way of its finitude. The decision to devote one's time to mastering Russian to read Dostoevsky in the original means one will have less time to spend reading about the history of mass transportation or grading student papers or playing with one's children or, of course,

---

26 This rejection of a distinct eternal realm led Kant to characterize Judaism (not admiringly) as "a religion without religion." See Michael Mack, *German Idealism and the Jew* (Chicago: University of Chicago Press, 2003), 23–41.

smelling the flowers. (It's worth remembering that Mendelssohn was both a congregational rabbi and an academic philosopher for most of his working life.) We cannot do everything ourselves: therefore, we must depend upon others — become part of an ongoing community — so that others might spend their time doing what we cannot, just as we spend our limited time witnessing, knowing, and doing what our fellow community members are unable to get around to themselves. The choice to do or think or make one thing rather than another that constitutes the particularity of an individual is meaningful only in the context of a finite lifetime:

> Since man's capacity is limited and therefore exhaustible, it may occasionally happen that the same capacity or goods cannot simultaneously serve me and my neighbor. Nor can I employ the same capacity or goods for the benefit of all my fellow men, or at all time, or under all circumstances. (*J*, 48)

Where for Locke, individuals were most perfectly themselves so long as their mode of self-expression remained belief, unrealized in the temporal world, Mendelssohn's individuals are particular only insofar as they exist at a particular time and place in history, and, so located, choose or have no option but to do one thing and not another with their limited time. Mendelssohn goes on: "Time constitutes a part of our property, and the man who uses it for the common good may hope for compensation from the public purse" (*J*, 60–61). Having been rendered finite, the individual human lifetime ceases to be what it was for Locke, the conceptual span within subjects manifest their capacity to do and make anything and hence to live as if forever, and becomes, for Mendelssohn, a material resource in and of itself.

It is this finitude of the individual human lifetime, its status as a resource that can be used up, moreover, that becomes the basis for Mendelssohn's fundamental redescription of the relations between Jewish and Christian conceptions of religious truth and the models of authority and sociability that ought to follow from those models. For Locke, we recall, subjects effectively join a socius, if not quite civil society, by expressing their identities as subjects by way of the things they make and possess and the beliefs they profess — by way, that is, of materializing their inner states and hence rendering them public and universally apprehensible (and also vulnerable to being stolen). Within Mendelssohn's notion of the lifetime as a limited material resource, by contrast, individuals are brought into social relation not because they experience a common material world, but because they don't. He explains:

> Our lifespan is not sufficient for us to experience everything ourselves and we must, in many cases, rely upon credible fellow men; we must assume that their observations and the experiments they profess to have made are correct. But we trust them only insofar as we know and are convinced that the objects themselves still exist, and that the experiments and observations may be repeated and tested by ourselves or by others who have the opportunity and ability to do so. (*J*, 92)

By dispensing with the notion that either the eternal world or some state of eternal belief ought to be understood as an analogue to and perfection of the temporally fleeting and contingent material world, Mendelssohn lays the groundwork for the coexistence of several sorts of religious truths, a coexistence that for him undergirds the possibility of the non-contradictory coexistence of a secular state and Jewish public. In the first section of *Jerusalem*, Mendelssohn aligns himself with a by-then familiar discourse of Enlightenment Deism, as he describes the existence of a world governed by natural law — that is, a world in which human and non-human elements are understood to be legible by virtue of their regular and predictable qualities. The truths of this natural world are not the special province of any particular religion, but are knowable by way of humans' exercise of their rational faculties, the possession of which defines the essential humanness of humans. Mendelssohn follows the cue of the Deists in defining this rational engagement with the truth of the world as "natural religion"; a state of belief whose terms, as

Elisabeth Weber puts it, "are inscribed in the soul with a script that is legible and comprehensible at all time and in all places."[27]

Where Mendelssohn departs from his Deistic predecessors is in his insistence that natural law need not comprehend the entire truth of the world; alongside the ongoing truths of natural law exist the specific truths of what he terms "revealed legislation"(*J*, 95). For the Deists, revelation by definition runs counter to the concept of natural religion, since it conceives of a truth the knowledge of which is restricted to the Almighty God up until the time and place that God chooses to reveal that truth to mere mortals. For Mendelssohn, by contrast, revelation need not contradict natural law or the natural religion available to all rational thinkers because *what is revealed is not truth, but legislation*. Judaism "knows of no revealed religion in the sense in which Christians understand this term" (*J*, 95). Where Christianity is organized around divine revelation, subjective states of belief including "doctrinal opinions," "saving truths," and "universal propositions of reason" (for the Deists, eternal truths of natural religion are present in creation itself and are therefore intelligible to everyone), Judaism is constituted essentially as a system of "divine legislation" — "laws, commandments, ordinances, rules of life" (*J*, 97). This divine legislation is revealed not to everyone but only to the people actually present at the moment of revelation, and in that sense has the status of an historical truth. People who were not present at the moment of revelation must depend on the testimony of those who were actually there.

Most straightforwardly, Mendelssohn seems to be suggesting that because no single person can experience everything that ought to be known, communities are constituted out of the interdependence of different knowing subjects with one another. In his account of a culture forged out of the *differences* of subjects' experiences, Mendelssohn marks his departure not only from

---

27 Elisabeth Weber, "Fending Off Idolatry: Ceremonial Law in Mendelssohn's Jerusalem," MLN 122, no. 3, *Special Issue: The Letter and the Law: German-Jewish Perspectives* (2007): 522–43, at 527.

the Lockean framework of belief we have been examining but from social contractarian and communitarian discourses of the nation-state as well, discourses predicated upon, respectively, a common, if tacit, consent and the assertion of a shared history, the inhabitation of a world that is shared because it is (commonly) made.[28] Mendelssohn also suggests the ways in which a revised understanding of belief follows as a matter of course from this emphasis on the limited and disparate experiences of social subjects. Belief does not — or not only — matter because it is a privileged or singular mode of consciousness — an especially non-fungible and eternal mode of self-expression, a singularly true belief. Rather, belief matters because it is a description of the perfectly normal and everyday ways in which individuals depend upon other people for knowledge they themselves do not experience, trusting what they cannot witness.

Viewed exclusively within this context of the limited knowledge of a finite lifetime, Mendelssohn's characterization of belief would seem simply a kind of disenchantment. It sounds like an argument for the primacy of historical, empirical knowledge predicated on the assertion there is nothing but that. But if historical truth is something one must trust to the verification of others who witness it and is in that sense distinct from both philosophy's metaphysical truths (discoverable by reason) and the revealed truth that is the provenance of belief, for Mendelssohn, divine legislation does not simply announce the limitation of truths to historical witnesses who have the good fortune to be in the right place at the right time. Rather, Mendelssohn understands the legislative quality of divine revelation to offer a structure for both registering and transcending the essential historicism of such legislation. Toward the end of *Jerusalem*, he advances a notion of "ritual" as the essential practice of ceremonial law, a practice that foregrounds the ways in which Jewish

---

28 Bonnie Honig's account of a Jewish — and more broadly, a republican — tradition characterized by foreigners-as-state-founders and as revitalizing immigrants is apposite in this context. See *Democracy and the Foreigner* (Princeton: Princeton University Press, 2001).

religious practice ought to be understood as continuous with secular historicism. Mendelssohn's case for the imbrication of historicism and religion is premised, that is, on a shift on what counts as religion when we move from Locke's Christian salvation to Mendelssohn's Jewish practice. As Mendelssohn elaborates it, ritual, or ceremonial law, stands both as a recognition of the fact of a finite human lifetime and as an articulation of such limitation as a precondition for the legibility and meaningfulness of the world:

> The written as well as the unwritten laws have directly, as prescriptions for actions and rules of life, public and private felicity as their ultimate aim. But they are also, in large part to be regarded as a kind of script, and they have significance and meaning as ceremonial laws. They guide the inquiring intelligence to divine truths, partly to eternal and partly to historical truths upon which the religion of this people was founded. The ceremonial law was the bond which was to connect action with contemplation, life with theory. (*J*, 128)

The ritual functions simultaneously as a singular event and as a kind of linguistic sign, meaningful only in its repeated iterations over time. In each ritual they perform, Jews are acting historically, acting within a particular set of unrepeatable conditions that necessarily become part of the meaning of that practice and indeed of the practice itself. At the same time such rituals function as a kind of script, repeating and transforming a set of gestures or signs whose significance lies in their iterations and reiterations through time. Such a notion of ritual unravels any hard-and-fast distinction between an action or event in the world and a subject's knowledge or interpretation of that event. All acts are fundamentally acts of meaning-making, and, as such, are known as basically as they are made to happen. As a framework for understanding his conception of belief as a reliance on other people's witnessing, Mendelssohn's ceremonial law works to complicate what might seem at first to be a privileging of what he terms "historical truth," knowledge of the sorts of events that only occur once and in relation to which individuals are especially reliant on others for their knowledge. Within the structure of ritual, any absolute distinction between historical truths and eternal truths comes undone, as the singular and the serial collapse into one another.

Moreover, for Mendelssohn, this undoing of a clear line between action and meaning is what positions Jewish ceremonial law as a superior instrument for overcoming the idolatry to which all forms of belief are vulnerable. While Christianity had from the outset positioned itself as a corrective to the legalistic literalism of Jewish law — in the Pauline formulation, Christian belief recovers the essential spirit of a truth that had been lost in the Jewish propensity for unreflecting adherence to law, to the "dead letters" of a kind of legal formalism — in Mendelssohn's reframing, the Christian claim to access to an eternal and unchanging truth turns out itself to be a kind of literalism or idolatry. The eternal, unchanging quality of Christian belief, far from standing as evidence of access to a certain essential spirit, represents a kind of idolatry, a literalizing commitment to the notion that the immaterial might be instantiated and made permanent. By contrast, Jewish ritual or ceremonial law, insofar as it registers the irreducibility of truth to any finitude or particular moment of legibility, is conceived by Mendelssohn as an embrace of "a living mode of writing," a kind of figuralism.[29] So where Locke understood the material and the eternal realms to be fundamentally distinct from one another, the immateriality of the eternal sphere — Christian spirit — offering the possibility of a perfect equivalence of identity and its productions and worth protecting on precisely those grounds, Mendelssohn envisions a notion of ritual in which the organizing of the implacable stuff of history itself happens within time, deliberate projects of retrospection and prospection.

---

29 Weber and Jeffrey Librett are particularly lucid around this point. See Weber, "Fending Off Idolatry: Ceremonial Law in Mendelssohn's *Jerusalem*," *MLN* 122, no. 3 (2007): 522–43 and Jeffrey Librett, *The Rhetoric of Cultural Dialogue: Jews and Germans from Moses Mendelssohn to Richard Wagner and Beyond* (Stanford: Stanford University Press, 2005), 59.

Lest it not already be apparent from the account I've offered thus far, Mendelssohn's conception of communal ceremonial law is both predicated upon the existence of a community and functions to constitute something like a public. In registering the historical particularity of a given moment of revelation — some people were present to witness and to receive the giving of the law; others must learn of it secondhand, from those who were present — ritual or ceremonial law both distributes roles in recognition of the differences in peoples' historical location and requires that people act in specific ways whose significance lies in the fact that others have acted in those same ways in the past. Insofar as the ritual acts in question are performed by new people in relations to an unprecedented historical context, however, the acts are restructured — sometimes in ground-shifting ways, sometimes in more minor and less evident ways — by each new performance, with every enactment folding in new members even as it transmutes the existing public and its terms of mutual engagement.

As has likely become clear by now, the model of ritual or ceremonial law Mendelssohn details in the second half of *Jerusalem* bears little resemblance to the alignment of individual identity and belief central to Locke's conception of secularism and likewise implicit in Butler's notion of "Jewish resources." But if Mendelssohn's notions of "revealed legislation" and the public-constituting rituals that follow from such revealed legislation challenge Butler's contention that the publicness of Zionism marks a radical departure from centuries of Jewish diasporic modes of subjectivity, it is still not clear how the kinds of publicness he describes might offer guidance for political governance, rather than just a description of how existing law works to build and organize publics. In order to find a model for governance within the description of ceremonial law, we need to look more closely at the laws governing the structure of publics themselves, not just the laws that such publics are charged with following. Although Mendelssohn does not explicitly evoke the discursive context in *Jerusalem,* the requirement that Jews assemble a *min-*

yan — a group of ten adults (not necessarily adults)[30] — for cer-

---

30 While the *minyan* is often understood to be a bulwark of exclusivist traditional practice — orthodox and *haredi* (ultra-orthodox) *minyanim* limit
their membership to adult males — the legal basis for such exclusions is far
from self-evident. In a position paper that served as one basis of the 1973
decision by the *masorti*/conservative movement to count women as part of
the *minyan*, Rabbi Phillip Sigel made the case that the legal grounds for limiting the *minyan* to men actually comes fairly late in the history of *halakha,*
or Jewish religious law. While the *Shulhan Arukh* explicitly states that the
"ten" required for the *minyan* are ten men, earlier codifications including
the *Mishnah* (*Megillah* 4:3) and Maimonides (*Mishneh Torah,* "The Laws
of Prayer," 8:4) only specify the number and not the gender, of the members. Sigal cites this history in order to make the case that the exclusion of
women was a *minhag* — a cultural practice or precedent — rather than a law.
Other members of the 1973 law committee who voted in support of count-
ing women in the *minyan* rejected Sigal's claim that limiting the *minyan* to
men ought to be seen as a tradition rather than a legal practice, suggesting
that the existing of dissenting voices did not a tradition make. These rabbinical scholars argued that while the weight of tradition and traditional
authorities opposed the inclusion of women, such inclusion nevertheless
could — and should — be justified as a *takana,* a repair, designed "to correct
an injustice or to improve the religious and ethical life of the community."
One member of a committee convened in 1979 to review the 1973 decision,
David Weiss HaLivni, argued that the codification of the inclusion of wom-
en as law ought to come only after a generation of women had actually come
to understand themselves to be obligated to pray. (Because a *minyan* is the
required minimum to allow for the possibility of any public prayer, the issue
under discussion is not whether women are allowed to pray publicly, but,
rather, whether they are obligated to do so. Only when members of a *minyan* understand their participation to be not optional can the *minyan* fulfill
its designated function as a precondition for the prayer of the community
at large.) HaLivni's position is relevant to the ways in which different understandings of the nature of the authority of *halakha* or religious law, even
more than differences in actual ritual practices or broadness of inclusions,
differentiate the various organized movements of Judaism. In his analysis
of the evolution of the positions concerning women and the *minyan* of the
Committee on Jewish Law and Standards of the Rabbinical Assembly, Rabbi
David Fine insisted that readers resist the temptation to understand questions of inclusion simply as points along a spectrum of strictness or loose-
ness of adherence to a law. Conservative movement rabbis "must above all
be loyal to the historical spirit of the people which the *halakha* only attempts to describe. The law as it develops through history is the concretiza-
tion of the spirit of the people, and perhaps, of God's revelation. This is
the key distinction between Conservative (sometimes known as *Masorti* or

tain ritual and liturgical acts has long been justified in both epistemological and representational terms. As the *Mishnah Megilla* (4:3) explains, the word used for "congregation" — *eida* — comes from the verb "to witness," while the witnesses in question are the spies described in Numbers 13:1–15:41, chosen by Moses at God's direction from each of the tribes of Israel and charged with the task of scouting out the nature of the Land of Canaan and its inhabitants. (Having just fled generations of slavery in Egypt, the Israelites in question have yet to encounter Canaan firsthand.) Returning after forty days, all twelve spies are in agreement about the unprecedented fertility of the land, but ten of the twelve insist that the inhabitants are giants, much too formidable to be confronted, while the remaining two argue that with God's guidance, the land would be inhabitable. When the report of the ten spies leads the wandering Jews to complain about Moses and demand that an alternative leader return them to captivity in Egypt, God is angered, and insists that, instead of entering the land they so fear immediately, they continue to wander in the desert for forty more years, one for each of the days the scouts explored Canaan. In the aftermath, the spies who advised against entering the land die in a plague, while the two dissenters, Caleb and Yehoshua Ben Nun, remain alive.

By insisting that a minimum of ten people be assembled for matters of public ritual, the rabbinic authors of *Mishnah Megilla* suggest that the fundamental religious unit is not the individual believer, but, rather, a ritual unit that is doubly heterogeneous, both drawn representatively from a range of preexisting social groups (one spy for each of the tribes) and sufficiently large to

---

Traditional Judaism) and Reform Judaism as they first developed. Reform Judaism sought to uncover the original pristine Prophetic Judaism before it became oppressed with talmudism and medieval rabbinism which reflected the nature of an inward-looking ghettoized Jewry. Conservative/*Masorti* Judaism, on the other hand, argued that there is no pristine original essence of Judaism which can be uncovered by a careful reading of the Bible and ancient history. On the contrary, the essence of Judaism is the experience of the Jewish people through history. The essence of Judaism is fluent since it develops through time" (Rabbi David J. Fine, "Women and the Minyan," Committee on Jewish Law and Standards of the Rabbinical Assembly, n.p.).

allow for a range of empirical experiences as well as a range of interpretations of those experiences. While rabbinic commentators largely follow the tonal cues offered in the original passage in Numbers — the spies are described as "traitorous" even as they are invoked as the basis of the *minyan* — the fact that the Israelites who take seriously the recommendations of the majority of the spies by demanding a new leader to return them to Egypt do in fact remain outside of Canaan, the express desires of both God and Moses notwithstanding, suggests that the *minyan* carries within it an implicit argument for democratic decision-making. (This conclusion would seem consistent with the requirement made explicit in the Biblical text that a spy be drawn from each of the tribes.[31]) The structure of the *minyan* in this way functions as a registration of the epistemological limits imposed by the historicity of experience and as an instrument for compensating for, without really transcending, that historicity.

But the heterogeneity of the *minyan* is not understood to function simply in epistemological terms. For some commentators, its importance lies in its operation as a structure of governance. The multiple perspectives the *minyan* enfolds can be useful at arriving at a fair valuation of something (as, for example, a plot of land) while Rambam suggests that the practice of praying in a *minyan* allowed public readers well-versed in the relevant texts to read for the benefit of the illiterate.[32] An explicit case for collective governance (as opposed to collective ritual practice) is first laid out in Exodus 18:1–20:23, where Moses' father-in-law Yitro becomes concerned that the leader has become overwhelmed by the task of adjudicating all disputes within the community, and advises him to appoint a committee of administrators to help him with the task of organizing the people. The medieval commentary on that same portion, known as *Itturei Torah,* generalizes Yitro's lessons by explaining that no Jew can fulfill all of the commandments of the Torah: some can only be fulfilled by priests or Levites, while others can

---

31 Parashat Yitro, *Itturei Torah,* vol. 2 (Jerusalem: Yavneh, 1987).
32 Maimonides, *Mishneh Torah,* "The Laws of Prayer," 8:8–9.

only be fulfilled by those who own houses or fields. As a consequence of this division of labor, all people must consent to be governed, because only as a collectivity are Jews capable of fulfilling all of their covenantal responsibilities.

In this regard, the Jewish Sabbath might be seen as paradigmatic, both in its centrality to Jewish ceremonial life and in the way it makes explicit its own dynamics of historicity and recurrence. In Locke's vision, the imperfection of labor — the ways in which individual agents alienate and lose themselves in the labored effort to express selves in material forms — can be repaired only in the realm of the eternal, where belief is a perfect and unappropriable expression of the self. In the *Kitab al Khazari* (*Book of the Khazars,* completed around 1140) the medieval philosopher and poet Yehuda HaLevi reminds his readers that they are to understand the Sabbath as "m'ayn ha'olam ha'ba" — "a taste of the world to come." In this vision the material world of labor and the condition of completion are not ontologically distinct realms, analogies of one another, but instead are separate but recurrent temporal moments, pulses in a cycle of days that both repeat and differentiate. It is the goal of producing a condition like the Sabbath that the week's labor is directed, but it is only because that condition can be repeatedly experienced that it is able to function as a condition of aspiration.[33] This requirement follows from Judaism's status as a system of laws, HaLevi explains. Given that ethics are to be evaluated in terms of behaviors rather than the beliefs or intentions underlying or producing such behaviors, behaving ethically becomes a matter of practice, in both senses of the term: the things one does, and

---

33 In a letter to German anti-Zionist Benno Jacob written in May 1927, Jewish philosopher Franz Rosenzweig celebrates the spontaneity of expression afforded by Sabbath observance in Tel Aviv, in which "all stores close from *kiddush* to *havdalah*" (the respective ceremonies marking the beginning and the end of the Sabbath), even as "the Zionists smoke, write letters and arrange sporting events." See Braiterman, "No *Parting Ways,*" 373.

the things one does over and again so as to do them better and better.[34]

My project up until now has been to show the ways in which both Butler's argument — anti-Zionism isn't anti-Semitism (and is therefore a legitimate, indeed persuasive, political position) — and her methodology — if Jews (or "Jewish resources") express hostility or ambivalence about Israel, the position is not anti-Semitic — are built upon an identitarian logic that borrows from a Christian conception of belief. Such an account, I have been arguing, fails to register the historicism and mundaneness of Jewish ceremonial law and ritual life, and the collectivism of Jewish practices that follow from such historicism and mundaneness. But a fundamental question remains: What follows politically from the demonstration that the collectivism and law-centeredness of Jewish life are not simply late innovations of European Zionists writing at a moment just prior to that period in which the visionaries and bureaucrats of European colonialism would come to recognize that their centuries-long project had run its course? What does the longer historical arc of Jewish

---

34 Even as the structure of Shabbat (Sabbath) offers itself as a formal structure within which individual practitioners come to see themselves as capable of becoming better and better at following a given law, it also builds in recognition of the possibility of failures of law-following. In the legal category known as *shevut* laws (from the same root "sh–v(b)–t" as Shabbat) rabbis detail ancillary laws that prohibit behavior that would not be forbidden on its own terms, but which is forbidden because it is likely to lead to prohibited behavior. So while the playing of musical instruments is not considered a violation of the Shabbat in and of itself, because such instruments might break, leading the player to be tempted to repair them, playing itself is forbidden in order to foreclose the temptation. Similarly, riding animals is not strictly forbidden on the Shabbat, but because one might be tempted to break a branch off a tree to urge the animal forward and that branch-breaking would count as prohibited behavior, animal riding is forbidden so as to stop the chain of temptation before it starts. What the existence of the *shevut* laws makes apparent is the degree to which law, particularly the law surrounding the Shabbat, is conceived as a mode of practice rather than a doctrine. For details, see the opening chapters of Maimonides' *Mishneh Torah*, "The Laws of Shabbat."

I'm grateful to Dvora Weisberg for her expert guidance on these aspects of rabbinic law.

collective life imply for the pressing and seemingly intractable political conflict in Israel/Palestine?

If the notion of the *minyan*, with its members drawn anew from various sectors for each and every ceremonial occasion and charged with the task of compensating for the inescapable limits and divergences of one another's experiences, can be seen to model the representative aspect of a kind of republicanism, in the provisionality and iterativeness of the Sabbath and ceremonial law, we can discover, I want to suggest, republicanism's process, the shufflings and reshufflings of a parliament's coalition politics. After all, such coalition politics are predicated on the notion that alliances are provisional, brought into being not only by the contingent emergence of overlapping interests but by the equally contingent and debatable discernment of such overlapping interests. They are predicated on the notion that policies that seem wise at one historical moment may come to seem deeply misguided at another, or might come to be seen as having been foolhardy (or evil) all along. They are predicated on the notion that the political meaning of a given coalition at a given moment is made possible and is made legible in relation to past coalitions and the intimations of future ones; that the particular membership of a given party at a given time might alter that party's sense of its interests, vulnerabilities, capacities.

The ways in and degree to which Jewish law ought to form the basis of the laws of the Israeli state was the subject of a great deal of debate immediately prior to the formation and in the early decades of the State of Israel. While much of the Israeli legal system was borrowed from the British common law system in place in Mandatory Palestine, advocates for a revival of Jewish law made the case for separating such law both from orthodox Jewish religious practice and from the British legal system. The language of rabbinic law was often introduced as a means of translating British legal concepts into the nascent modern Hebrew language, but early members of the Supreme Court were divided as to whether this language should function simply as an instrument for naming British concepts or whether the complex legal concepts and debates within the Biblical and

Talmudic legal traditions ought in certain cases to take precedence over British law.[35] Simcha Assaf, a rabbinic scholar without formal training in any modern Western legal tradition, was appointed to Israel's first Supreme Court so that he might offer expertise in Jewish law; in the years since then, there has generally existed an informal "religious chair" on the Supreme Court, though most occupants of that chair since that time have been trained in both systems of law.[36]

More significantly, Ronen Shamir has detailed the brief flourishing of the now largely forgotten "Hebrew Law of Peace," a community court system pointedly distinct from existing religious institutions within the *Yishuv* (pre-state Palestinian Jewish community) envisioned as a step toward permanent establishment of a secular legal authority undergirded by both historically shared communal practices and the existing body of Jewish legal scholarship. Both the orthodox religious establishment and the British mandatory government resisted the establishment of such a court system — the orthodox rabbinate because such a system threatened their monopoly over the power to interpret and make sense of religious texts; the British because the establishment of community courts ran against their colonial strategy of centralizing authority. After the British passed the 1922 "Advocates' Ordinance" regulating and professionalizing the training of lawyers, the Hebrew Law of Peace Movement and its nascent institutions largely faded away.[37]

---

35 Shimon Agranat, "Jewish Law As Reflected in the Decisions of the Supreme Court of Israel," *Dine Israel* 5 (1974); Assaf Likhovsky, *Law and Identity in Mandatory Palestine* (Chapel Hill: University of North Carolina Press, 2006).

36 Michael Dan Bernhack and David Nosraski, "Jewish Seat, Minority Opinions and Legal Pluralism" [Hebrew], *Legal Minutes* (June 1999): 499–542. Thanks to Assaf Likhovski of Tel Aviv Law School for his help on this topic.

37 See Ronen Shamir, "The Hebrew Law of Peace: The Demise of Law-as-Culture in Early Mandate Palestine," in *The History of Law in a Multi-Cultural Society: Israel 1917–1967*, eds. Ron Harris, Alexandre Kedar, Pnina Lahav, and Assaf Likhovski (Aldershot: Ashgate, 2002), 110; and *Colonies of Law: Colonialism, Zionism and Law in Early Mandate Palestine* (Cambridge: Cambridge University Press, 2000).

We might thus see the demise of the Hebrew Law of Peace system as a missed opportunity, a path marked out and then wandered from in the push-and-shove of colonial political skirmishing. Ultimately, however, my argument does not rise and fall simply upon the actual historical role of Jewish law in the Israeli legal and political systems as they are currently constituted. Rather, I am inviting us to read the structure and mode of practice of Jewish ceremonial law *formally,* not as a set of directives about how to be a member of a specific spiritual community of people known as the Jews, but as a model for imagining how groups of people might craft the intelligibility and value of a world as conscious relations to past efforts to make the world valuable and intelligible, and might understand that effort to offer a structure for inhabiting that world with others at a given time. In making the case, then, that the possibility of discovering many of the structures of democratic practice within Jewish ritual and ceremonial law undoes the neatness of the distinction between Zionism and Judaism upon which Butler rests her argument, I am decidedly *not* arguing that the democratic tradition discoverable within Jewish thought ought to be understood as offering a model for Israeli democratic practice limited only to its Jewish citizens. If Mendelssohn's *Jerusalem* presents a framework for discerning the existence of a republican tradition within Jewish thought and practice well in advance of the establishment of the State of Israel's first parliaments, the attentiveness of such a tradition to the contingency of political boundaries, to the historicity of political value, suggests the possibility of reading a history of Zionist aspiration whose accomplishment need not be measured exclusively, or even primarily, in relation to the civic status of Jews.[38]

---

38 In her March 2004 Tanner Lectures, delivered at Berkeley and later published under the title *Another Cosmopolitanism* (Oxford: Oxford University Press, 2006), political theorist Seyla Benhabib identifies a dynamic of "democratic iteration" she calls "jurisgenerative politics," which she defines as "cases of legal and political contestation in which the meaning of rights and other fundamental principles are reposited, resignified and reappropriated by new and excluded groups, or by the citizenry, in the face of new and

If, as I am suggesting, we can discern the contours of repub-licanism[39] within at least some traditional conceptions of Jewish ceremonial law and ritual, the state in which that Jewish repub-

---

unprecedented hermeneutic challenges and meaning constellations" (148). Benhabib takes as her central illustration "L'Affaire du Foulard," the series of encounters between French-Muslim school girls committed to wearing the hijabs mandated by Muslim religious law to the public schools they attend-ed, and the public school and government officials who saw the presence of scarves in the public sphere of the school to be a violation of the French republican investment in maintaining a "state neutrality" toward religious symbolism. (The series of confrontations began in 1989 and continued spo-radically for much of the following decade.) While most analysts of the af-fair historicize the clash by noting the ways in which postcolonial waves of immigration exposed the political limitations of the long-articulated French commitment to universalism, revealing such commitments to have rested upon a no longer sustainable presumption of a homogeneous French citizenry, Benhabib, evoking terms reminiscent of Mendelssohn's double ac-count of ceremonial law, is invested in tracing the productive "disjunction between law as power and law as meaning" (49). By way of a series of demo-cratic iterations in which the repeated use of terms or concepts do not pro-duce replicas of original meanings or usages but transformations, "the girls and their followers and supporters forced what the French state wanted to view as a private symbol — an individual item of clothing — into the shared public sphere, thus challenging the boundaries between the public and the private. Ironically, they used the freedom given to them by French society and French political tradition, not the least of which is the availability of free and compulsory public education for all children on French soil, to trans-pose an aspect of their private identity into the public sphere" (53), trans-muting a religious symbol into a symbol of conscious political defiance.

39 In *Democracy and the Foreigner* (Princeton: Princeton University Press, 2003), Bonnie Honig traces a discursive history of "the symbolic politics of foreignness," making the case for a tradition of a republicanism in which the foreignness of founders, immigrants and citizens is not exceptional but constitutive of a republican political sphere. Honig analyzes a number of narratives from the Hebrew Bible as they are appropriated and reframed through various iterations: the Moses of Exodus mutates into the Egyptian Moses of Freud's *Moses and Monotheism*; the foreigner-as-immigrant in the Book of Ruth is rewritten and transformed by Cynthia Ozick and Julia Kris-teva. Philip Pettit, by contrast, imagines a version of republicanism in which the heterogeneity of a given state's population works to mitigate the op-pressiveness of state coercion, a coercion Pettit understands to be necessary to protect citizens' capacity to participate in the public sphere. See *On the People's Terms: A Republican Theory and Model of Democracy* (Cambridge: Cambridge University Press, 2012).

lican tradition has come to be instantiated exists within — and has operated to produce — geopolitical circumstances that make it imperative that the version of republicanism established in the State of Israel incorporate Jews and non-Jews in full equality. I have been arguing that the forms of republicanism within Jewish practice describe both the practice of politics — ceremonial law with its shifting, jurisgenerative alliances and meanings — and its mode and reach of representation — the *minyan*. The narrative from which the concept of the *minyan* is drawn carries within it an ambiguity, an ambiguity that registers, I want to suggest, a careful awareness of the appeal and the dangers of political self-determination. While the narrative of *Shlach Ľcha* (Numbers 13–15) traces the activity of twelve spies, representing each of the twelve tribes of Israel, the number drawn from the story as the minimum necessary to count as a ceremonial public is *ten* — the number of spies who *agreed* with one another as to the dangers of entering the land and whose position is later excoriated. We might understand this slide from the original witnessing group of twelve to a public of ten in at least two ways: first, as offering the model of an ideal public, in which the public's boundaries constitute and are constituted by an essential unity and homogeneity of opinion; and second, as articulating a minimum understood as a *floor*, the lower limit by which to assure the existence of a political community defined by its heterogeneity, by a defining diversity of opinion. Rather than choosing definitely between these two interpretations, I want to propose that we read the irresolution of the *minyan* form as a tension meant to be sustained, an acknowledgment both of the enduring allure of political purity, and of the importance of resisting that allure over and again.[40] With the *minyan*, the pleasure of

---

40 In my 2012 book, *The Moment of Racial Sight* (Chicago: University of Chicago, 2012), I trace the dynamics of nineteenth-century British political philosopher John Stuart Mill's discomfort with moments of political resolution. In contrast with the *minyan*, in which the group is the foundational unit, Mill's central concern is the disposition of individual political subjects. He worries that, given the central role played by political debate in sharpening individual citizens' judgment and powers of discernment, once a policy

inhabiting a political community in which other people agree with you need not be disavowed entirely. Rather, that pleasure of like-mindedness needs to be experienced with the knowledge that it cannot — and indeed ought not to — last. By acknowledging contingency and temporariness as the defining qualities of political community, citizens of the *minyan* have reason to treat their political opponents as people who will likely at some not-too-distant future moment, be their political allies.

This presumption of ongoingness also creates a deep sense of the connection between the process of advocating for one's visions and interests and the carrying out of the visions, the realization of those interests, in ways that emphasize the continuity of the polity's legislative and executive functions. Within the Israel of its pre-1967 borders, both Arab and Jewish citizens possess the right to vote,[41] but parties that identify themselves as non-Zionist are not included in ruling coalitions.[42] (These parties are mostly Arab parties, but sometimes include parties representing ultra-religious and non-Zionist Jews as well.) What this means in practice is that while the implicit support of

---

within a given political community has been arrived at and is no longer subject to debate, the citizens who follow that policy simply because it is established legal practice (or convention) lose the opportunity to develop and exercise their own critical faculties. While Mill suggests that organizing one's engagement with the world by way of different combinations of sensory faculties can work to keep individual subjects' powers of political judgment well-honed, in place of offering the promise of an ever-mutable material world, the *minyan* structure envisions a political community that is always on the verge of becoming a different one. See Irene Tucker, *The Moment of Racial Sight: A History* (Chicago: University of Chicago Press, 2012), ch. 3.

41 Peter Beinart, in his 2012 *The Crisis of Zionism,* suggested the Israel within the green line be termed "democratic Israel." See *The Crisis of Zionism* (New York: Times Books, 2012).

42 In recent years, as hopes for a two-state solution have faded and Israeli Arabs have seen their own civil rights erode, a significant number of Israel's Arab citizens have opted to boycott the Israeli elections in which they are eligible to vote, understanding their participation to be an endorsement of an unjust political system. See Sherry Lawrance, "Arab Nonvoting in Israeli Elections: To Boycott or Not?," https://www.academia.edu/203500/Arab_Nonvoting_in_Israeli_Elections_To_Vote_or_Not.

non-Zionist parties for a given coalition can sometimes enable that coalition to ascend to and remain in power — in the years immediately following the signing of the Oslo peace agreement, the coalition led by Prime Minister Yitzhak Rabin was kept in power by such an implicit arrangement — MKs from not-quite-official coalition member parties are prohibited from serving as cabinet ministers.[43] (They are allowed to serve as deputy ministers, and a member of a non-Zionist Arab party, Ahmed Tibi, currently serves as deputy speaker of the Knesset.) The effect of this arrangement is to create an absolute split between the executive and representative functions of government, a split at odds not only with prevailing theories of republicanism but with the interconnection of *minyan* and ceremonial law I have been describing. A parliamentary system organized along the lines of the republican tradition I have identified, one that understands the contingency of alliances as a generative condition of political relations rather than a quality to be expelled, would eliminate the requirement that parties identify themselves as Zionist in order to serve as members of a governing coalition.

The more complex and politically significant implication of a reading that distinguishes a history of Jewish democracy from the particular history of the Israeli state concerns the question of who precisely ought to be eligible to vote. Once we identify republicanism itself as a recurrent element of Jewish communal practice, the political system currently in place in the occupied territories, in which Jewish settlers possess the right to vote and Palestinian residents do not, is indefensible not only from a human-rights perspective but represents a renunciation of the very cultural tradition right-wing advocates of a "Greater Israel" purport to be instantiating. Squaring the circumstances of the occupation with the republican tradition I have identified will

---

43 For the history of Israeli parliamentary coalitions and their relation to executive power, see Danny Korn and Boaz Shapira, *Koalitziot* [Coalition politics in Israel] (Hebrew) (Modi'in: Zmora-Bitan Publishers, 1997); Danny Korn, "The Presidentialization of Politics: The Power and Constraints of the Israeli Prime Minister," Joseph and Alma Gildenhorn Institute of Israel Studies, Research Paper 2, March 2010.

require the Israeli state to reconstitute itself in one of two ways. On the one hand, it can limit the right to vote to voters living within the internationally recognized boundaries of Israel, requiring Jewish settlers who choose to live east of the Green Line to cede their right to participate in Israel's democratic processes for as long as they remain outside the state's borders. (In this regard, settlers would be treated similarly to Israeli citizens living outside the country: with the exception of those Israelis living abroad on official government business, Israeli citizens must return to residences within Israel if they wish to vote. There is no such thing as absentee voting.) If Palestinians living in the occupied territories are denied the voting rights enjoyed by Israeli Arab citizens living within Israel's official borders, then the rule of law demands that Israeli Jews be treated the same, so as to mark the distinction between legally accepted and contested Israeli territory.[44]

Alternatively, the Israeli state might opt to continue to allow the settler population living in the occupied territories to vote, but if it chooses to do so, the "Jewish republicanism" I have identified would require that the vote be extended to all Palestinians living there, a population orders of magnitude larger than the

---

44 It is worth noting that by most estimates, limiting the vote to citizens living within sovereign Israeli territory would have altered the outcome of the 2009 elections in which Benjamin Netanyahu and his Likud coalition came to power. In that election, Likud won 27 seats, one fewer than the 28 seats won by Tzipi Livni's centrist Kadima party, but because right-leaning parties won more seats overall in the election. Netanyahu was given the first opportunity to form a government. David Makovsky, an analyst for the Washington Institute for Near East Policy, estimated that without the settler votes, Likud's seats would have fallen to 26 and Kadima's rise to 29, making it overwhelmingly likely that Livni, not Netanyahu, would have been asked to form a government. See David Makovsky, "Imagining the Border: Options for Resolving the Israeli-Palestinian Territorial Issue," The Washington Institute for Near East Policy, http://washingtoninstitute.org/ pubPDFs/StrategicReport6.pdf; Nitzan Goldberger, "West Bank Settler Voting Trends, 2006 and 2009," Settlement Report 19, no. 4 (July/August 2009), http://www.fmep.org/reports/archive/vol.-19/no.-4/west-bank-settler-voting-trends-2006-and-2009; quoted in Beinart, The Crisis of Zionism, 217–18.

population of Jewish settlers. Such a configuration resembles the "one-state" solution advocated by the Butler of *Parting Ways* and other advocates of BDS. To the degree that the Jewish republican tradition I have identified is understood in purely formal terms, there is nothing to recommend either of the two possible structures over one another. But my goal in demonstrating the possibility of finding a tradition of republicanism in the seemingly remote Jewish practices of the *minyan* and ceremonial law has not been merely to point out the tradition's authorization within Jewish practice. Rather, I have been committed to showing how Jewish practice offers a particular reading of republicanism, one that conceives of the mechanism of republicanism as an engagement with the historicity of public life, a structure that registers and attempts to compensate for the irreducible heterogeneity of experience and values, of power and vulnerability, of an always changing population. Within the context of a republicanism that takes historical contingency as its motive force, not just a condition to be overcome, there are no triumphant conclusions to be drawn. An argument — my argument — in favor of one dispensation over another will not take the form of a stepwise demonstration of superiority, but rather a series of tentative speculations, "likely-tos" in places of QEDs. By that measure, the case to be made for the version of republicanism that withdraws voting rights from Jewish settlers in preparation for a two-state solution over the version of republicanism that grants rights to West Bank Palestinians in preparation for a one-state solution is simply that the first is more likely to result in a functioning, relatively civic political life, one less burdened by destructive internecine wars and the distrust born of more than a century of conflict. The former solution acknowledges the centrality of the recent and incommensurate traumas and vulnerabilities, of anger and destruction of and by Israeli Jews and Arabs, of and by Palestinians in Gaza and the West Bank, of and by Palestinians and Jews scattered in Europe and the Americas, by offering a framework for building two political spheres that allows two peoples to step away from one another for a moment, to step away in order to build, a step on the way to a possible future of reengagement, of thick and vibrant heterogeneity. It is a gesture of political modesty, a vision of civic life that engages the insurmountability of the past by refusing, for the moment, to try to surmount.

Bibliography

Agranat, Shimon. "Jewish Law As Reflected in the Decisions of the Supreme Court of Israel." *Dine Israel* 5 (1974).

Altmann, Alexander. *Introduction to Moses Mendelssohn, Jerusalem, or On Religious Power and Judaism*. Hanover: Brandeis University Press, 1983.

Azoulay, Ariella. "Declaring the State of Israel: Declaring a State of War." *Critical Inquiry* 37, no. 2 (Winter 2011): 265–85.

Batnitzsky, Leora. *How Judaism Became a Religion*. Princeton: Princeton University Press, 2011.

Beinert, Peter. *The Crisis of Zionism*. New York: Times Books, 2012.

Benhabib, Seyla. *Another Cosmopolitanism*. Oxford: Oxford University Press, 2006.

———. "'Ethics without Normativity and Politics without Historicity': On Judith Butler's *Parting Ways: Jewishness and the Critique of Zionism*." *Constellations* 20, no. 1 (2013): 150–63.

Bernhack, Michael Dan, and David Nosraski. "Jewish Seat, Minority Opinions and Legal Pluralism," [Hebrew] *Legal Minutes* (June 1999): 499–542.

Bilgrami, Akeel. *Secularism, Identity, and Enchantment*. Cambridge: Harvard University Press, 2014.

Bilgrami, Akeel, and Jonathan Cole, eds. *Who's Afraid of Academic Freedom?* New York: Columbia University Press, 2015.

Braiterman, Zachary. "No Parting Ways: The Crypto-Zionism of Judith Butler." *Political Theology* 16, no. 4. Special Issue: Forum on Judith Butler's *Parting Ways* (July 2015): 371–77.

Brown, Wendy. *Regulating Aversion: Tolerance in the Age of Identity and Empire.* Princeton: Princeton University Press, 2006.

Butler, Judith. "Judith Butler's Remarks to Brooklyn College on BDS." *The Nation.* Feb. 8, 2013.

———. *Parting Ways: Jewishness and the Critique of Zionism.* New York: Columbia University Press, 2012.

———. "Response," *Political Theology* 16, no. 4. Special Issue: Forum on Judith Butler's *Parting Ways* (July 2015): 392–99.

Cooper, Julie E. "A Diasporic Critique of Diasporism: The Question of Jewish Political Agency," *Political Theory* 43, no. 1 (Feb. 2015): 80–110.

Fine, Rabbi David J. "Women and the Minyan," *Committee on Jewish Law and Standards of the Rabbinical Assembly.* 1979.

Freudenthal, Gideon. *No Religion without Idolatry: Mendelssohn's Jewish Enlightenment.* South Bend: University of Notre Dame Press, 2012.

Goldberger, Nitzan. "West Bank Settler Voting Trends, 2006 and 2009," *Settlement Report* 19, no. 4 (July/August 2009), http://www.fmep.org/reports/archive/vol.-19/no.-4/west-bank-settler-voting-trends-2006-and-2009

Hammerschlag, Sarah. "Outside the Canon: Judith Butler and the Trials of Jewish Philosophy," *Political Theology* 16, no. 4. Special Issue: Forum on Judith Butler's *Parting Ways* (July 2015), 367–70.

Honig, Bonnie. *Democracy and the Foreigner.* Princeton: Princeton University Press, 2001.

Kolsky, Thomas A. *Jews Against Zionism: The American Council for Judaism, 1942–1948.* Philadelphia: Temple University Press, 1990.

Korn, Danny. "The Presidentialization of Politics: The Power and Constraints of the Israeli Prime Minister." Joseph and Alma Gildenhorn Institute of Israel Studies, Research Paper 2. March 2010.

——— and Boaz Shapira, *Koalitziot* [Coalition Politics in Israel] (Hebrew). Tel Aviv: Zmora-Bitan Publishers, 1997.

Lawrance, Sherry. "Arab Non-Voting in Israeli Elections: To Boycott or Not?" https://www.academia.edu/203500/Arab_Nonvoting_in_Israeli_Elections_To_Vote_or_Not

Lees, Yonatan. "Sof haMercaz Smola" ("End of the Center Left"). *Haaretz* (Hebrew), November 22, 2013, 7 (print).

Lennard, Natasha. "'Effective' Censorship over Israel Event at Brooklyn College." *Salon.* Feb. 4, 2013.

Levy, Gideon. "The Israeli Patriot's Final Refuge: Boycott." *Haaretz* (English). July 14, 2013 (electronic edition).

Librett, Jeffrey. *The Rhetoric of Cultural Dialogue: Jews and Germans from Moses Mendelssohn to Richard Wagner and Beyond.* Palo Alto: Stanford University Press, 2005.

Likhovsky, Assaf. *Law and Identity in Mandatory Palestine.* Chapel Hill: University of North Carolina Press, 2006.

Lloyd, Vincent. "Is Critique Theological?" *Political Theology* 16, no. 4. Special Issue: Forum on Judith Butler's *Parting Ways* (July 2015): 388–91.

Locke, John. "Letter Concerning Toleration" (1689) in *Two Treatises of Government and A Letter Concerning Toleration.* New Haven: Yale University Press, 2003.

———. *Two Treatises of Government,* ed. Peter Laslett. Cambridge: Cambridge University Press, 1988.

Mack, Michael. *German Idealism and the Jew.* Chicago: University of Chicago Press, 2003.

Maimonedes. *Mishneh Torah.* http://www.chabad.org/library/article_cdo/aid/682956/jewish/Mishneh-Torah.htm

Mahmood, Saba. "Can Secularism Be Other-wise?" in *Varieties of Secularism in a Secular Age,* eds. Michael Warner, Jonathan Vanantwerpen and Craig Calhoun, 282–99. Cambridge: Harvard University Press, 2010.

Makovsky, David. "Imagining the Border: Options for Resolving the Israeli-Palestinian Territorial Issue." *The Washington Institute for Near East Policy.* http://washingtoninstitute.org/pubPDFs/StrategicReport06.pdf

Mendelssohn, Moses, *Jerusalem, or On Religious Power and Judaism.* Hanover: Brandeis University Press, 1983.

Pettit, Philip. *On the People's Terms: A Republican Theory and Model of Democracy*. Cambridge: Cambridge University Press, 2012.

Reznik, Larisa. "Melancholic Judaism, Ec-static Ethics, Uncertain Politics." *Political Theology* 16, no. 4. Special Issue: Forum on Judith Butler's Parting Ways (July 2015): 382–87.

Sandel, Michael. *Democracy's Discontent: America in Search of a Public Philosophy*. Cambridge: Harvard University Press, 1996.

Scheer, Jonathan. *The Balfour Declaration: The Origins of the Arab–Israeli Conflict*. New York: Random House, 2010.

Shamir, Ronen. "The Hebrew Law of Peace: The Demise of Law-as-Culture in Early Mandate Palestine." In *The History of Law in a Multi-Cultural Society: Israel 1917–1967*, eds. Ron Harris, Alexandre Kedar, Pnina Lahav, and Assaf Likhovski. Aldershot: Ashgate, 2002.

——————. *Colonies of Law: Colonialism, Zionism and Law in Early Mandate Palestine*. Cambridge: Cambridge University Press, 2000.

Sullivan, Winnifred Fallers. *The Impossibility of Religious Freedom*. Princeton: Princeton University Press, 2005.

Taylor, Charles. *A Secular Age*. Cambridge: Harvard University Press, 2007.

Tucker, Irene. *The Moment of Racial Sight: A History* Chicago: University of Chicago Press, 2012.

Weber, Elisabeth. "Fending Off Idolatry: Ceremonial Law in Mendelssohn's Jerusalem." *MLN* 122, no.3. Special Issue: The Letter and the Law: German-Jewish Perspectives (April 2007): 522–43.

Yitro, Parashat. *Itturei Torah*, vol. 2. Jerusalem: Yavneh, 1987.

"W. dreams, like Phaedrus, of an army of thinker-friends, thinker-lovers. He dreams of a thought-army, a thought-pack, which would storm the philosophical Houses of Parliament. He dreams of Tartars from the philosophical steppes, of thought-barbarians, thought-outsiders. What distance would shine in their eyes!"

— Lars Iyer